REAL FRIENDS TALK ABOUT RACE

REAL FRIENDS TALK ABOUT RACE

YSEULT P. MUKANTABANA
AND HANNAH SUMMERHILL

PARK
ROW
BOOKS

PARK
ROW
BOOKS™

Recycling programs
for this product may
not exist in your area.

ISBN-13: 978-0-7783-8705-3

Real Friends Talk About Race: Bridging the Gaps Through Uncomfortable Conversations

Park Row Books
22 Adelaide St. West, 41st Floor
Toronto, Ontario M5H 4E3, Canada
ParkRowBooks.com
BookClubbish.com

Printed in U.S.A.

I dedicate my words to all my Black, Brown and people of color who may find solace in this book. To all people who want genuine, loving and compassionate friendship because it's a power we have been neglecting while in thrive of a better future.

For Dave

TABLE OF CONTENTS

INTRODUCTION

**What do you think of when you
hear the word *friendship*?**

For me, friendship is something that evolves and grows as we grow and evolve as people. At its best, it supports and guides us, and at its worst, it can be toxic and can take from you emotionally and mentally. Just like intimate relationships, friendships need boundaries and constant care to flourish. They're a reciprocal union that should be genuine, kind, and compassionate. I also wholeheartedly believe that friendships can and should sometimes break if they do not respect and nurture a safe and healthy environment. Friendships don't have to be perfect—they never are!—but they need to have a healthy basis to work from and both sides need to want the best for the other person.

In any close relationship, we come to it with our own issues: our self-esteem and past wounds caused by other people in our lives. But I've found that the ideal friendship offers a safe space to try to be the best human we can be in this world, in times of strength and also, in moments when we feel the most vulnerable.

I personally have had the blessing of curating an amazing group of remarkably close and loving friends—most of them are friendships that I've had for ten to twenty years. I really pride myself on how long they have lasted and how healthy they are. I grew up moving around a lot and a great fear of mine was that I'd become a person that didn't have old friends—people I could laugh with about the ridiculous things we did in our twenties. I had to adapt and learn how to stay in touch—nurture these friendships virtually and on the phone because I wasn't always with my friends in person. Now that my friend group has scattered all around the globe—in Africa, Europe, and the Middle East—I get invited all over the world to gather and celebrate with these special people.

I also now make it a point to hold space for new friendships, like my friendship with Hannah. She and I met at an odd time for me, when I wasn't planning on adding more people to my friend group. When we met, I did not instinctively think we would be friends. She had recently started to do anti-racist work and I appreciated her efforts to be an ally. I also appreciated that she didn't make me feel like I had to be the Black girl that would guide her on her allyship journey. That's a lot of pressure to put on a new friendship, and I was grateful Hannah didn't put me in that position.

As a white person, is there anything more uncomfortable than talking about race and racism, even with your closest friends? Sex, religion, and politics all seem easier than the conversations about race we *should* be having. Even though most of us want to be seen as our full selves in close relationships, which includes all that makes up our identities, we avoid having productive conversations on race. Unfortunately, our society—our schools, churches, and workplaces—have ill-prepared us for these dialogues, the kinds that could lead to real progress. As white people, we avoid them because they're difficult, uncomfortable, and because acknowledging our differences only scratches the surface of what lies beneath even our most benign cross-racial interactions: our harmful history, our society's obsession with whiteness, and our individual responsibility.

For those who are looking to broach the race conversation with their friends, but don't feel equipped with the tools, context, or confidence to do so, we aim to give you those resources with this book. Our goal is to transform the ways that people of color and white people relate to and understand each other, because there is no justice or equity without conversation, first.

In both interracial friendships and same-race friendships, there should be space to talk about race. I mean that for white friendships, too—as white people, we are not raceless, and our silence about racism contributes to an inequitable society, whether it's intentional or not. After creating space for these kinds of dialogues in our work as the Kinswomen, we've seen firsthand how deeply healing and bonding having these conversations can be. The vulnerability it takes to share and be witnessed in all that makes up our identities creates stronger, more fulfilling friendships across our differences—even though they may require extra care and consideration.

Honesty is such a big part of my friendship with Hannah, I hope that our transparency will give space for conversations that often don't come naturally—specifically within interracial friendships. I've seen firsthand when my Black or POC[1] friends realize that they've never had these conversations with their white friends, and by the time they're having them, they realize there's a big gap in understanding. For me, it's like an elephant in the room if these conversations don't come up with my

---

1   People of Color.

white friends. It's like I'm not acknowledging a huge part of me that makes me whole. I also know from being friends with white people that there are situations that come up—comments, attitudes, and the like—that remind me we're not living in the same type of reality. I think having these kinds of conversations should be a natural, common practice of friendships.

I think the biggest reason why it's so hard to talk about race in friendships, even really strong friendships, is fear—the fear that our differences will be too great and talking about race will kill the "good vibes." It's natural to be afraid to talk about something that you worry will distance you from someone you love so much. It *is* scary because there are no real tools that account for the complexity of being friends or in love with someone who says something problematic or has racist ideas.

I have felt a great deal of shame when I've found myself in those dynamics. I felt responsible, like I had failed myself by putting myself in spaces and interactions that ended up being offensive and damaging both mentally and emotionally. There's always the potential of losing a friend or experiencing the anguish of white fragility, a response that tends to shift blame and cause even more harm.

The reality is that interracial friendships are layered and require a different kind of emotional labor. I want to be clear that I never want to pressure BIPOC[2] into having interracial friendships or make it seem that they're required to do the work to "teach" their white friends about racism. I understand all too well the anguish and hurt that these cross-racial interactions can cause, and I want to honor that. I understand that as people of color, we don't all have the same bandwidth or desire to learn how to navigate this. There are moments when I want to tap out and just take refuge in spaces where I feel seen and understood completely, without having to teach to anyone. That to me is okay, too, and it is necessary.

---

2   BIPOC stands for Black, Indigenous, and People of Color.

Another challenge to having these conversations is that some people think that because friendships form across racial lines, it's a testament that racism is dying. While that would be nice to believe, proximity in the form of friendships or romantic relationships to BIPOC does not prove white people are allies or that we've transcended a racist society. The kind of conversations we're hoping to foster also pushes white people to be accountable for the harm they cause—even if unintentional—and to make real changes in their lives. It forces people to take applicable action to make a real shift in themselves. Done well, I think these conversations would make friends and lovers feel closer and allow for a more genuine kinship. I feel safer knowing that I can talk about these issues with my white friends because they are able to see me in my whole experience of this world. I can be open and tell them when I have experienced something hard outside of our friendship knowing I'll have their support.

Yseult and I are always aware of the racial power dynamics that exist in our friendship, and we're conscious of how our partnership is perceived. Our conversations and our work together as a Black woman and white woman reveal the tension, trauma, and discomfort that are often present between white people and people of color. This tension and its fissures are obvious everywhere—on social media, in pop culture, in our knowledge of and perception of history. All of this to say—interracial friendships and relationships are not necessarily easy, nor are they an indicator of a post-racial society.

How did Yseult and I get here in the first place? We met a few years ago at an event about bridging the gaps between women of color and white women, where attendees were free to approach the mic and share their perspective or personal experience. I sat in the back quietly, but when Yseult got up to the mic, she pointed out, exasperated, the lack of participation from white women like me who'd attended an event that was explicitly about cross-racial dialogue. I realized I'd completely missed the point: I was acting as a voyeur instead of being vulnerable. When I saw Yseult again several days later, I recognized her instantly. She's striking—tall, beautiful, and a little intimidating. (A true Scorpio, as I'd later come to realize: hard shell but soft on the inside.) But I introduced myself anyway and asked if she wanted to continue the conversation. I wouldn't be quiet this time. Yseult agreed.

I did agree. I usually have Tupac's quote ringing in my head when something unexpected happens: *"Don't trust nobody."* But this time, I let my gut decide, and I shooed off the thought. If anything, continuing the race conversation with Hannah would be a social experiment, and I'd have a good story to tell my friends. But Hannah had good energy and huge eyelashes that clapped together every time she blinked. I thought she looked like Bambi, so I said yes. I was skeptically optimistic.

I had no idea what our podcast *Kinswomen* would become, but I was inspired by the conversations we were having and felt the need to bring these untold narratives to a bigger audience. I wanted to help create a space where other women of color like me could safely talk about the racism we experience in everyday situations and feel heard by the white women in our lives. So often anti-racism work is centered on white people, and I think it's essential for BIPOC to have a space to talk about our experiences and understand our own legacy and its effects. To be honest, I knew nothing about podcasts at the time, but a friend of a friend offered to produce it, and I was excited by the opportunity.

When Hannah and I first created *Kinswomen*, it felt like we were meeting our real selves for the first time. We had a good and healthy rapport early on, even though I knew little about her. As we continue to grow in our business, we are also caring for our friendship, one I believe in and cherish. As in all friendships, there are ups and downs, and we have had our share of both.

★ ★ ★

We wanted to spotlight this, but we also wanted to create a welcoming space, one that shows compassion to the friends and listeners choosing to engage in these complex conversations. Our platform and podcast, *Kinswomen*, is aimed at building trust between women of color and white women, and for white women specifically, accepting the discomfort and pain that comes with growth. When we create space to articulate what is often unsaid, or what we believe to be shameful or taboo about race, we can move through this world with more empathy and a better impact on those around us. The cross-racial conversations I've been privileged to be part of have changed me and my friendships.

I want the same for you, no matter how you identify. In this book, we'll share our framework for building trust across racial lines. We'll talk about the covert and overt ways that racism shows up in our interpersonal relationships, and for white readers, how to take radical responsibility for our impact.

Recently my friend Leslie offered an analogy about hardships in general, which resonated with me in thinking about my friendship with Hannah. Hashem (G-d[3] in Hebrew) talks about the crushing of olives as the materialization of hardships and challenges in our life, and that what comes from the crushing of the olive is oil that we use to light the wick of a candle, which represents our soul. The hardships and challenges are what gets us closer to our soul and truest selves. Even when we experience hard moments, it's these moments that bring us closer to knowing who we are. I thought it was a beautiful

---

3   Due to Yseult's religious practice, she doesn't spell out the full name of the Holy One.

    Chabad.org explains: "Following the Torah's instruction to 'obliterate the name' of idolatry in the Land of Israel, the Torah warns us not to do the same to G-d. We thus learn that there is a prohibition to erase G-d's name. Writing G-d's name could lead to erasing or disrespecting G-d's name."

idea to hold on to when I experience difficult or uncomfortable moments in life and in my friendships.

It's juicy for any reader to know that we want to be genuine and forthcoming about the things we experience in our business together and friendship. It was an important aspect for us to be open and share our experiences honestly. I hope that our transparency will give space for conversations that don't come so naturally—the ones about interracial friendships.

This type of conversation pushes white people to take accountability and not just stay stuck in what they might "sound or look like."

What white people must really let go of in these conversations is the idea of perfection. As we discuss later on in the book, perfection is a toxic idea that does two things that I find so harmful: it makes white people think they must be "right" all the time, and thus gives no space to learn and be vulnerable. I have no expectation that white people are supposed to be experts at everything, especially for things outside their experience. I expect white people to be open and up front about their own shortcomings, which helps restore the balance and equality of our humanity that isn't allowed for in white supremacy.

Being friends with a white person while also having to name what's wrong and staying true to myself can be exhausting. I'm also the kind of person who feels intensely about things—that's part of my personality. A healthy and open interracial relationship means that the white person has to listen to their friend and not make everything about themselves. It's so simple, but I've had my share of experiences that suggests it's actually not that easy. In the case of my friendship with Hannah, I can talk about anything, and if something weird happens between us, I call her in and we chat. I don't feel like I have to guard my heart all the time because she is doing the work, and she agreed to the interracial friendship clause when we met. In return, I'm patient and kind with her and always speak from love and openness. We have built trust and understanding by being open and honest with each other about everything.

In our own friendship, Yseult has pushed and challenged me to expand my narrowed white, American lens. Her words haven't always been easy for me to hear. You, too, may feel discomfort, resistance, or denial when engaging in this work. Keep reading, and we'll get you through it together.

As a white woman, I am in no way an expert on race or racism, and I never will be. Everything I've learned that I write about in this book, I learned from BIPOC. Allyship is a lifelong journey, and it requires continuous education and action. It also comes with a steep learning curve for most of us. I value truth, justice, and equity—like most people—but there's a huge difference between saying so and living like it. I wanted to cowrite this book to help us bridge the gap between having knowledge of inequity and taking action to abolish it. It's a goal I'll be forever working toward. If you're white like I am, you might feel more comfortable, at first, reading my words than reading Yseult's, or other Black authors and educators. But as a white woman, my voice should not be your guiding voice in anti-racism. As you continue on your allyship journey, diversify your education as much as possible. Listen to the experts. Don't stop here.

My wish is that this book provides the first step—a glimpse of hope and light in your interracial relationships. I hope that this book can center our humanity, as a way to restore hope for both BIPOC communities and white people wanting to be on a journey of allyship. We need to normalize how hard it is to be close to white people, in the same way many women[4] express how hard it is to be friends with men.

---

4   When we use "women" we are inclusive of all people who identify as women.

I'm not foolish enough to think I hold the ultimate truths or points of view in talking about race, but this book is a good starting place to learn how to have the often-uncomfortable dialogues about interracial friendships. We need to remember that we are friends first; that means we need to be kind—especially from the white person in a position of learning how to unpack things that will feel deep and incredibly uncomfortable. I have learned that there's true liberation in getting comfortable with discomfort, especially when you are in a position of self-reflection and change.

I want this book to feel incredibly uncomfortable and comforting at the same time! Like when you have a weird rash on your arm and when you ask your friend if they've ever had it, and they respond yes. It makes you feel better that they are not dead from it. It should feel like a possibility of a conversation starter and something people can come back to because they feel seen and understood in our words. My dream is that this book gives language to sentiments that people have felt but could not find the words to articulate.

ONE
The Kinswomen

Origins

Before we get into the work of building trust in interracial friendships, it's important for us to share a bit about our backgrounds. As a Black woman and white woman growing up on opposite sides of the globe, we've seen the world and have *been* seen by the world with very different eyes. Like all relationships, we bring to our friendship context, history, and perspectives that are important to acknowledge.

I find it important to show that having a balanced interracial relationship doesn't mean only focusing on what makes us the same, but also what makes us different. This fights the false narrative that a good interracial friendship is where the "minority" assimilates and does everything to make the white partner feel comfortable and seen at all times. I think it's healthy to reexamine that dynamic and what it means today.

I grew up hearing and seeing minorities being praised for "integrating"—meaning accepting everything that's white as the baseline and norm.

Diversity is true wealth. It's my goal to offer a version of ally-ship and friendship that shows what it's like to not make yourself small and "assimilate" to a status quo that doesn't align with the core of who you are as a BIPOC person. I want this book to help equalize what it means to be in an interracial friend-ship, and for it to be a reminder that no member of a histori-cally marginalized community must feel like there's a part of them that needs to be erased.

Yseult

From where my life started, I could never have predicted where I'd be today. Sometimes, I sit back and try to trace how things could have been or where I could have ended up. Everything that makes up my story is special to me. I can't help but get emotional thinking about how my grandmother would feel knowing how far I've come. I promised her I'd make a legacy of our names and story, to carry my culture and values to people who may not know where my country is on a map.

I don't want to pull on emotional strings, but I do feel emo-tional opening up about myself and my story. I had humble be-ginnings being born in Bujumbura, the capital city of Burundi, the neighboring country to Rwanda. I wasn't able to go back home to Rwanda[5] until I turned eighteen years old.

My mother had me as a teenager and relied on my grand-mother to help. She later fell in love with the man who would become my father. He was from Belgium, and they were both young when they met. He rocked long hair and had a motor-

---

5   Due to Rwandan history, my grandmother had to flee in 1959 for her safety. She fled to Burundi, where she had to rebuild her life. It was only after the 1994 Genocide against the Tutsi that the diaspora was able to return.

cycle, on which they decided to get married. Literally: someone made them husband and wife as they sat on his motorcycle.

Soon after getting married to my father, my mother had Ricky, my first sibling. I was five years old at the time. Burundi was beginning to enter into a civil war that would last for ten years. My parents decided it would be best to move our growing family to Belgium.

I don't remember how I felt at the time, but I can imagine how a five-year-old not speaking anything but Swahili felt arriving in a place like Brussels. I was quickly expected to learn French and assimilate to my new life and environment, away from my grandmother and family back home. It was then that I met my father's family: they were all white and Belgian. I soon realized I didn't look like the other kids in my father's family and was made to understand those differences through situations that a child doesn't necessarily understand but feels.

After three years in Belgium, my parents decided to move to Irving, Texas. My dad was going to study for two years, getting his master's in business, and we all went with him. I attended a local school and learned English pretty fast. After he finished his MBA, we returned to Belgium.

While our various moves were the right thing for my family, having to learn and excel in two new languages in the span of five years was something that started to reflect in my school performance. My parents wanted me to fit in and do well, but thinking back, I remember leaving Texas having a fifth-grade level of English and returning to Belgium with a third-grade level of French. I had to pick back up where I left off, and catching up on those few years missed in French was really rough.

I can vividly remember trying to learn a French tense called *passé composé* ("past tense"), which is a tense that describes actions done in the past and emphasizes its results in the present. I felt like my brain was broken. It was just not computing. Those next few years took a toll on my confidence and self-esteem. There was also a heavy sprinkle of racism that made the whole ordeal so hard on me and my parents to navigate within the school system. The entire school system was based on student rankings—type 1 to 8, which was meant to cater to children with various learning abilities. Type 8 was for children that struggled with dyslexia, had trouble paying attention, or had dyscalculia, for example.

I was placed in the type 8 schooling, and my parents worried I wouldn't have a normal and fruitful education as a result. My parents knew this was based on a misunderstanding of my capabilities and fought, especially my mother, tooth and nail to place me in a different ranking. Here were white teachers claiming to know how smart her Black child was, and she was not going to let the West dictate how much her child was capable of.

It's important to note that the ways the school measured my intelligence were drenched in racist ideas, with zero willingness to consider that my travels and learning two languages in such a short time might have had an influence on my difficulties in school. Today as an adult, it's amazing to see how narrowly I managed to beat the odds of students who come from the "Individualized System" in Brussels, where many encounter dead ends educationally and professionally. The number of students who leave the system and enter a "normal" high school is 1 percent. I couldn't find any statistics on how many of these students went on to earn a university degree, but I'm guessing the number is very small.

As a result, I felt immense pressure to prove to everyone that I wasn't a statistic and to make sure I honored the fight my parents had to get me into a different ranking. My parents also hired a *logopède*, which translates as a speech therapist, to help me transition to schooling in Brussels. The person my parents chose was a lady named Anne, and she was so kind and patient. We saw each other each week to sit and play; at least it felt like play. She facilitated games that were meant to fortify my educational foundations in all types of subjects.

Our sessions together gave me space to be vulnerable. She redefined the meaning of school and learning. I felt smart leaving her room, and her teachings restored a sense of confidence that those few years of being bad at everything had completely annihilated. I had felt like everything I did was wrong and ending up in that "individualized school" made me feel like the dumbest little girl in the room. I felt like I had failed my mother and father and was the shame of my family. Working with Anne was the moment that pivoted my whole educational experience. My parents had invested in something that changed my life. I felt confident to finish and ended up in university like I had always wanted for myself.

The issue is that unfortunately everything is tainted with xenophobia and racism. It seemed that they targeted me, or at least were quick to judge a non-white child's difficulties, as unfit to stay in the traditional system.

My own experience is nothing unique for many minorities in Belgium, many coming from second or third generations of immigrant parents, who are struggling with language barriers and busy making a life for themselves. This dynamic makes it so that many minority students are flushed out of the traditional system because parents don't really know how to fight it or, I suspect, can't imagine that their kids are being treated this way because of racism.

I grew up being subjected to racism, but if someone was raised in a land where they were the majority, they aren't automatically going to see or recognize racism when it happens to them. I remember the first time my mother told me she was confused by something racist, and her confusion came from having never previously experienced racism. What's so upsetting is that many of my peers in Belgium were smart, capable students that could have had another trajectory than the one they ended up on. The system they lived in wanted to cut short their possibilities. I mean, can you know how beautiful and tall a flower can be if you cut it too early? Children are sources of endless possibilities and should be taught in that way. Today in my thirties, I understand that my mother's roar saved me from being eaten up by a system that didn't take seriously my capabilities. And this formative experience taught me early that I wasn't permitted to make many mistakes and that my struggles would be seen as incompetence. It's a feeling and experience that stays with me today, and I understand viscerally the double standards and treatment of BIPOC.

Right after high school, my father and mother asked if we wanted to move to the US. I was so excited; it had been a struggle living in Belgium. If you were bullied every day for years, you would despise the place that let it happen. I'm only human. There was little to no representation of minorities in most career paths, and there was a major extreme-right Flemish party that was gaining more and more support every year. Socially, I couldn't shop or dine without having a staff member disrespect me. The whole experience of living there was mentally and emotionally exhausting. Of course, racism exists in the US as well, but in Belgium you are gaslighted into thinking that you're exaggerating or being ungrateful for speaking up.

At the time I didn't have the words, but these microaggressions take a toll. They sit with you for a long time. I hated feeling like I didn't do or say enough when these racist incidents happened. And I could never understand how someone could see something and say nothing. White people around me would always turn to me to do a little "solidarity shrug," raising their eyebrows as if to say, *"What can we do?"* so that I knew they weren't the racists in the room. But aren't you just as problematic if you say and do nothing? It's as if someone got beat up in front of you and you patted them on the shoulder. That's first-class solidarity! I'm not a pointless hater; this comes from personal experience. Emotional boundaries are applied to absolutely everything for me. This is all self-preservation. I decided a long time ago that abuse, no matter how normalized it becomes, should never be accepted.

Finally, in 2008, we made the big move back to the US after having lived ten years in Brussels. I've been here for thirteen years now. I live in New York and have two degrees: one, a BA in Interpersonal Communication, and the other, a master's from the School of Hustle that NYC forces you to acquire if you want to survive. The US has its own demons, but here, I hold strong self-power and solidarity to be able to defend and preserve my humanity.

The foundation of my inner strength has come from my beautiful and amazing family, in particular the women in my family. My aunts, mother, and grandmother are their own world. While I was growing up, I watched them; they exuded confidence and fierceness that inspired and nourished my soul with self-love. They were all so graceful and displayed a natural deep sense of resilience and power. I just wanted to be loved and held close by them so I could imbue myself with their grace and light.

I would get so excited when my aunts and grandmother would visit when I lived in Brussels. They would all sit together with my mother and start chatting and laughing, reminiscing about their younger years. When my grandmother was around, she would chime in and had a laugh so contagious you would find yourself laughing, even if you didn't know why. My grandmother had an unspeakable level of grace that I pray to have one day. As soon as she entered a room, she inspired immediate respect. All she needed to do was to look over when I was making too much noise for me to feel her reproach. I remember how she would go to bed the same time I would even if she wasn't tired because I was afraid of the dark. That was the kind of grandmother she was.

Another loving and important figure in my life is my aunt, Tata Fatou. A naturally intimidating woman, she's tall, slim, and has exquisite posture. My aunt sits with her head held high with arms crossed, her superlong legs extended; her posture is a manifestation of her energy and grace. Each time I knew I was going to see her, I made sure I looked impeccable. She has an eye for detail and doesn't hold back on telling you if you look like you just got out of bed. She expects you to look presentable, speak clearly, and hold yourself erect. In fact, as I'm writing this, I just sat a little straighter. I won't lie, Tata Fatou still intimidates me today, but in the most loving and empowering way.

These things that I picked up from my mother and Tata Fatou have influenced how I see myself in this world and my expectations for myself and other people. They have made me become a woman that knows what she wants and demands nothing less. I have become unapologetic about absolutely everything that I claim to identify myself, as a Rwandan, Jewish, lesbian woman and so much more. I discovered late that I was gay, and it didn't feel like I had a big reveal to share; I felt secure and comfortable with my new reality. Everyone close, my aunts, cousins, and parents, didn't flinch; they just embraced my reality. Or when I discovered that my soul is Jewish, I told my parents and everyone just embraced it. They all said that the only thing that matters is that I am happy. I felt no shame, no resistance to dive into my true self.

When my mother and aunts would have nights out, they would walk out beautiful and elegant every time; it's as if they were moving synchronized in slow motion. I would look up in complete awe. I felt like Simba in *The Lion King*, in the scene when he looks up at his dad as they look over their kingdom. I loved watching them laugh in complete freedom and fill the room with an energy I couldn't experience any other place. They all carried their experiences of grief, hardship, and wins in their own ways; all of them seemed to have decided to thrive the best they could. I'm not sure that they realize how much their presence made an impression on me, but these women were the foundation of my self-worth as a young Black girl in a white world that constantly tried to make me feel like I wasn't worthy.

Because of them, I understood where I came from and know where I am going and why I'm on my journey. I bring along all that I am: Rwandan, Jewish, Black, and queer, with all the culture and insight that that means for me and my heritage. I was taught young that in order to know where we are going, we have to remember where we are from. These women in my life personify parts of where I am from, and they remind me that my existence isn't simply a person navigating racism. They restore humanity that I need. I want people who read this book to internalize the idea that there are many stories and points of view that are worthy of learning from.

My greatest hope for this book is that pieces of my story will maybe make BIPOC feel seen and better understood. And for white readers, for them to be able to understand that white supremacy has been lying to them and giving them a false narrative that doesn't at all reflect the realities of BIPOC—both their neighbors and others far out in the world.

Hannah

Yseult and I share a birth year: 1987, but that seems to be where our childhood similarities end, at least on the surface. Unlike Yseult, who grew up navigating new continents and new languages every few years, the geography of my upbringing was limited to a few city blocks. I was raised in Allentown, Pennsylvania, a city somewhere between Philadelphia and Amish Country, speaking one language: English.

My hometown found fame as the subject of the 1982 Billy Joel song "Allentown," an anthem for the working class that found themselves out of a job when Bethlehem Steel shut down in the late '70s. Allentown's mayor at the time called it a "gritty song about a gritty city."[6]

My family (my parents, my two younger sisters, me, and our beloved pet rat, Zuffy) lived in a row house in a neighborhood with blocks of them, where the pharmacy, my friends' houses, my schools, and the midwifery center where I was born were all within a three-block radius. Our street housed mostly white families, including ours. Even though I often felt self-conscious about our humble dwellings, I loved where we lived. With all my friends in such close proximity and my best friend living just up the street, we could all play in the back alley behind our houses and go from yard to yard without ever straying too far.

My father was a writer, and my mother worked at local theaters, doing their marketing and publicity. They met working at a magazine company that my mother had relocated from Michigan to work for. My parents keep a pile of *New Yorkers* on either side of their bed and play Scrabble together at the kitchen table—East Coast intellectuals. Proud Democrats, and hard workers. Watching them parent the three of us, I remember their dedication to us, and their exhaustion. Our yearly vacation was spent driving to Michigan to visit my mother's parents, whom we adored. My parents placed a big importance on the arts, and my sisters and I each got to participate in one extra-curricular activity. Having spent so much time at the theater for every take-your-daughter-to-work and sick day with my mom, I chose acting classes at the local community theater, Civic. I loved that its name was a palindrome like mine.

The underfunded middle school that I attended one block up from where we lived was what other, whiter school districts would consider rough. Statues of gargoyles overlooked the entrance. Students who received in-school suspension were banished to the top of the school's towers. The building had no

6   https://www.mcall.com/news/mc-xpm-1992-12-27-2880003-story.html.

campus and was situated on a city block, so when we'd have to evacuate for bomb threats, we'd all line up on the sidewalk outside people's homes. The school, and my memories of it, have a gothic filter.

Even though the school population was mostly students of color, the city being home to large Puerto Rican and Black communities, the school was heavily segregated. In the cafeteria, the teachers ruled like dictators. Our assigned tables were called up one at a time to get our food, based on how quiet and "well-behaved" we were being. If we were too rowdy, we were punished with a Silent Lunch. It was at this school where I first recognized the racial divide between me and my classmates.

Unlike in elementary school, in middle school we were sorted into our classes based on our test scores. In sixth grade, the smartest kids were placed in 6-1, the next smartest was 6-2, and so on until 6-10. At lunch, we were only allowed to sit with those in our specific class level. The 6-1 table of students was mostly white, and then, moving through the cafeteria toward the 6-10 table, the tables got progressively less so. The same proved true the next year, where I was placed in 7-1. Though as a white student I was a minority at the school, I was placed at the top of the ladder, ranked literally as number one. I can only imagine the impact the not-so-subliminal message of our school's numerical ranking system had on our young minds.

At home, my family did not discuss race. We were a "colorblind" household. My sister Ariel often talked about a boy in her ballet class that she had a crush on—I'll call him Brian—and I'd tease her about him. I remember picking her up from class and seeing Brian for the first time. I was around seven at the time and I said simply to my mom on the drive home, "Brian's Black." I hadn't expected him to be.

I remember my mom whipping around from the driver's seat, mad at me. "I *love* that your sister is color-blind!" She was actually crying, so angry at me for noticing the color of Brian's skin.

It was my first major (misguided) Race Lesson. I interpreted her reaction to mean that it was impolite to notice that others were different, and that *Black* was a bad word. I never forgot that moment, and for many years I felt proud of my mom for being so, in my mind, progressive.

My parents were well-intentioned white people, like a lot of their friends, and they raised my sisters and me to be the same. Racists were always Other People, and those people were bad. It felt good to live on that moral high ground.

Middle school is where so many of us begin to learn the rules of social hierarchy, and it was no different for me. I remember the first instance I spoke up after witnessing what I perceived to be injustice. It happened in the cafeteria, of course. A shy girl was sitting alone, getting food thrown at her from a neighboring table of students. She kept perfectly still as they taunted her, and looked down at her plate silently. The teachers did nothing. I remember saying to the table of kids, "Stop throwing food at her!" They retaliated by throwing food at me, but I'd felt brave, like I'd done the right thing.

Thinking about it as an adult, the bitter irony is that injustice was happening all around me, not just to my fellow white classmate. Only the kids from the lower-scoring tables were being punished and as a result missing class for in-school suspension. We were learning history exclusively from white teachers. At eleven and twelve, it was almost as if our fates were decided— our middle school rankings not just a marker for how likely we'd be to succeed in society, but also how closely we appeared to conform to society's norms. I still keep tabs on my classmates from my class. They all seem to be doing well. As for the others, I don't know. I didn't get a chance to know them; we were literally segregated.

Hearing Yseult's stories of being a young girl experiencing racism in her school system while white adults looked the other way breaks my heart in half. I cannot imagine so many being witness to trauma in action and doing *nothing*, and what it might feel like to process that as a young girl. We hear stories like Yseult's and imagine that we will never be the adults who turn a blind eye. But the reality is that we are turning blind eyes all the time, and our negligence is violence.

As white people, I think we avoid talking about race due to a mix of ignorance and fear. At the very least, it feels uncomfortable. Even though those are not reasons to opt out, I pretty much did for decades. I believed that existing as a color-blind "open-minded and liberal" white woman was enough, and that my impact on people of color was neutral, if not positive. Maybe you, too, can relate to that point of view.

Race is still a topic that most white people have never had proper education on, but in which we consider ourselves experts and have *lots* of opinions. Paradoxically, most white people also consider themselves raceless, and therefore blameless when it comes to racism. When we *do* talk about racism, we are rarely implicated in the cause or responsible for the solution.

I'd like to ask you to embrace the discomfort you might experience while reading this book. Whether the feeling is a constant companion or it sneaks up on you, please don't let it prevent you from moving forward. We'll be talking about race, racism, white supremacy[7], and interracial relationships, and we'll make references to white people. As a white woman, I include myself within that group, and I am not using the word pejoratively. If you're like me, and you've been socialized to avoid talking about race, expect awkwardness and discomfort to be present while you read this book, and possibly *forever*, when it comes to conversations on race and racism.

As a human, and as a woman with white privilege and so many other privileges, I want to have a positive impact, especially as I learn about the destruction that whiteness has wrought

---

7   White supremacy means that anyone existing outside of whiteness has been relegated to second-, third-, or fourth-class citizenship.

and continues to create. As an adult, it's my responsibility to educate myself on the history that was absent from my schoolbooks, and to unlearn the lies of white supremacy. In this book, we'll also discuss the gaps between who we imagine ourselves to be as white people and what our actual impact is on those around us.

Perhaps you can relate to my story: you grew up avoiding the subject of race out of politeness or fear; you received subtle and overt messages about racial hierarchies from school, your community, and the media; and as an adult, you feel too uncomfortable to even begin to have open and honest conversations about racism, even though you desire to have a positive impact.

So, how can we begin to have productive conversations about race *and* have a positive impact when racism seems like an insurmountable evil? It starts on the person-to-person level. For me, it started with my friendships.

Friendship Beginnings

Hannah and I met when she approached me after I spoke at an event on cross-racial dialogues at The Wing, a members-only social club for women. The Wing's short-lived success was met with a wall when staff started speaking up about their treatment from management and members. In the brief time I was there, I had noticed how dysfunctional and racist the place was. I wrote to the management about it, and they sent a white girl who was the head of Community to speak to me. She eagerly thanked me for speaking to her, but soon after, I learned she was also super problematic.

I didn't want to stop being a member, because I really loved how safe I felt there as a woman. I liked The Wing for its physical comfort, cuteness, and women-focused space, but I could read the room. The women acted like they were sitting on the lap of a unicorn emoji. The place felt like an Instagram filter, and in each corner of the room, you could have a week's worth of photo content for your posts. But things didn't feel right. I could see through the fake smiles and *"Hiiii's"* that had way too many *i*'s to be real. The majority of the white girls were acting like they'd paid for a modern version of servants, throwing napkins and asking the predominantly Brown and Black staff to "get that." Occasionally, a white staff member would stare at me trying to figure out if I was a member—until I pulled out the member's card—and then they would give half a smile and welcome.

I wanted to try to help make the place better, by speaking up for myself and BIPOC staff and other members that were experiencing the same things. But I witnessed outright rudeness and lack of manners from white members. The staff were encouraged to give members the "princess" treatment: we could leave our dishes out and they'd come and pick them up, and they'd bring us whatever we needed. It was a high level of service that many members took advantage of to an abusive degree. The Wing's staff was mainly Black and Brown women, and they were required to serve these members no matter what was said or done to them. It seemed that all it took was a membership fee for the white members to feel entitled to a certain kind of treatment. I was livid by what I saw and became friends with a few of the girls that worked there, who confirmed what was happening.

Given the circumstances, it's funny that Hannah and I met at The Wing and ended up being close friends and working together, since the place has become synonymous with fake friendship and white feminism. I remember Hannah being friendly—the white type of friendly that doesn't make me feel entirely comfortable. I know most white people think of themselves as approachable, since they are never portrayed as scary by movies, TV, and the media. The movie *Get Out* was one of the first movies accepted by popular culture that managed to illustrate the hesitancy that Black people may feel around whiteness. I count myself in having a hard time trusting easily in spaces that are mostly white. Even though it's very much a horror movie, *Get Out* was classified as a comedy at the Golden Globes, but that deserves a whole other conversation.

At the time, The Wing felt like a petri dish of all the societal racial issues that existed outside of its doors that white feminism consistently ignores. They had successfully been able to materialize their whiteness into a massive white-centered, racist, functioning, and successful company that was all wrapped up in a pastel, pink-colored bow. Their majority white members could be problematic without anyone holding them accountable. There was no meaningful structure that encouraged decency and intentional anti-racist and anti-antisemitic behavior.

When we met, I hadn't considered what Yseult's experience as a woman of color at The Wing might be like. Most white people move through the world with so much ease that we don't recognize that that ease is such a privilege. Coming from my corporate, cubicle-grid life, The Wing was the most intersectional and feminist work space I'd ever been a part of. I couldn't see what was going on in plain sight as Yseult could. The Wing was started by white women, and often, we see only white men as the ultimate oppressor—never ourselves. This, I believe, was The Wing's downfall. But back then, the superficial optics supported my confirmation bias that The Wing was a great place for all women: Black hair-care products in the bathroom, the artwork on the walls depicting faces other than white women, messages of intersectional feminism everywhere I looked. Meanwhile, out of sight, in the kitchen, young white managers were demanding Brown workers give them massages.

It's also sobering to hear that Yseult was wary of me because it's a reminder of our two different realities. The way that I perceived myself as an unharmful, well-intended white woman was naive, in hindsight. Why would I expect that a Black woman would trust me instantly? (Probably because I was socialized to believe so.)

But back to when we first met:

When we met, I couldn't have imagined we would become close friends and business partners. Hannah and I are different in so many ways, but in the best ways as well. She has a bubbly energy to her. She's sweet and actually means it! Hannah is the type of person you see smiling at everyone, but I know it isn't fake. Our friendship is the only time that the saying "opposites attract" has been true in my life.

We didn't grow up in the same environment, and our energy vibrates differently, but I couldn't be more comfortable with her. Her whiteness isn't much of a challenge to our friendship, because she's so open to learning and understanding, and she's there for me when I feel drained. I give my all to be supportive in her journey to allyship, too.

Soon after The Wing event, Hannah began hosting conversations about race in her living room, and I attended the first one. She invited a few friends and set up some chips and wine for those that indulged. It was mainly white women in attendance, which I appreciated, because it would have felt weird to walk into a room full of BIPOC women at an event run by a white woman talking about race. I held back on speaking because I wasn't there to teach them—at least I didn't *want* to be the Black girl expected to teach everyone. I also was curious to understand what Hannah's motivations and intentions were for hosting these gatherings.

At that first meeting the discomfort was palpable, and some women seemed on the edge of shedding a few tears, which I apprehended greatly, because again, I didn't want to console anyone while potentially being triggered. But I observed that most people there wanted to learn or at least share how they felt. There was clearly a gap between what I knew and spoke about with my friends of color and these well-intentioned white people. And instead of pretending that they had all the answers, the women present were eager to learn and connect genuinely among other white people like them.

Right after I attended her first living room conversation, I left for Israel for a few months. I didn't really think of that conversation again until I realized Hannah had continued the meetups while I was gone. I kept receiving the invites, and she'd also been casually keeping in touch. I was pleasantly surprised that she had continued to create that space.

I find it frustrating when white allyship is this one-time effort meant to be a grand gesture that makes white people feel good about themselves for the year. Kind of like when you donate to that one ocean advocacy nonprofit so you can feel like you participated in making the world cleaner. *Performative* is the word of the year, and social media is filled with these ultimately empty gestures.

Hannah was different. It seemed like she was committed to hosting these conversations for herself and her white friends. When I got back from Israel, I wanted to meet with her again. I felt like we could have important conversations and connect on a deep level. I got the impression she would hold space for stories like mine, which would selflessly bring solace to my own heart and heal me from my experiences, but also be informative to others. I thought a podcast was a good setup to create a loving and compassionate space to hear narratives and offer a new way to have racial conversations.

I tend to do an "energy scan" when I'm around white people, to gauge the level of bullshit I'm potentially going to deal with. I don't see this as pessimistic, but rather realistic, because TRUST me, this is based on lived experience. I've had people try to befriend me so I could make their friendship look like a Crayola box, as if I'm some kind of brown crayon to add to their coloring book parties. A big thing that made me like Hannah was that she didn't tell me that she was married to a Black man. I remember learning Dave, her husband, was Black the first time I went to her place and as I was leaving her apartment, he was coming up. I realized then he was a BROTHER and a cool one at that. That was a major indicator for our potential friendship. Not because she was with a Black man, but because it hadn't been her letterhead of conversation.

I see my friends and intimate partner as an intentionally curated selection of people that bring something special through their own personality, but never to the detriment of my existence, which obviously includes my Blackness and Rwandan identity. I don't know that I can effectively explain the anguish I've felt having to let go of someone because of a race-related moment. It's not easy and it hurts, but it's also necessary for me to do to preserve my sanity and mental well-being.

It may read self-centered, but if I experience hardship and challenges from the outside world because of my identity as a Rwandan, Jewish, queer, and Black woman, I don't want to be preoccupied fighting for myself in an intimate space. Just like when you are a woman and you experience sexism in the streets and at work, the last place you want to experience that is at home or at a dinner party with your closest friends.

That's why it feels so special to find friends that meet that standard and bring that peace.

Yseult later asked me if it was intentional or not that I didn't mention that my husband, Dave, is a Black man, when we first met. It's not something that I hide, nor is it something that I'd ever lead with to give me "credibility" as a white woman. But Dave is the impetus for my journey of allyship in the first place—I wasn't one day sprinkled with woke dust by an antiracism fairy. Meeting and falling in love with him made it startling clear where the gaps in my empathy and education were.

It's a shame that it took falling in love with and living with a

Black person to see the world through his eyes and to recognize my own privilege. To be able to see white supremacy only when I saw up close someone who'd been victim to it is an example of my own willful blindness and white supremacy's trickiness—it's so pervasive and normalized that it almost seems invisible to white people.

I also know that having proximity to people of color does not make me an ally, nor does my marriage to Dave make me a "good" white person. Being with him has given me a much wider perspective, but it's still a limited perspective. As a woman, I was motivated to connect with women of color, too, and learn more about how I could bridge the gaps between us.

Even though Yseult seemed guarded when I approached her at The Wing, when she arrived at my apartment for our first meeting, she was *ready*. There were just a few of us—Yseult, myself, my white cousin, a couple of white friends who didn't really know what I'd invited them to, and a new friend, Frankie, a Black woman that I'd met at our wedding venue.

I set out bowls of chips and opened a few bottles of wine, each second wondering what I thought I was doing. Who was I, as a white woman, to bring strangers together to talk about race? The night could go so wrong. Who was Yseult? I barely knew her. Was Frankie only here because I asked her and she felt like she couldn't say no? Would she feel comfortable sharing her truth when I was technically a client of hers? Should I have asked her at all? Would all the pressure be on Yseult and Frankie as the Black women? Would I say something racist, accidentally? Would there be a fight? Tears? Laughter?

When everyone arrived, I took out a notepad and brought the meeting to order. I tried to be intentional about creating a container for the evening. Everyone seemed uncomfortable—everyone but Yseult. There was no nervous chatter or shifting in her seat. Her truth came out like a cannon and set the tone for the honesty, transparency, and force that would become the norm for these meetings. After that first meeting, there was an overwhelming sentiment: we need to do this again and again. Really, we need to always be doing this.

We started meeting once a month with our friends in my seven-by-seven windowless box of a living room. There was a group of regulars. Yseult, along with my friend and coworker Sandy—who founded the Black employee resource group at my company—always showed up without fail and ready to get into it. I had the opportunity to hear how women of color felt without filter, on a regular basis, for the first time in my life. I was blown away by what I was hearing, and what I *hadn't* been listening to. The truth had always been there, but it felt like I'd been living a parallel life from my friends of color.

In the beginning, it was hard to get a consistent group together, and the responsibility of what I'd created began to get to me: Who was I to create this space? What if I said the wrong thing or offended someone? What if only one woman of color showed up and the white women expected her to answer all the questions? What if only one white woman came and disappointed all of the women of color? All of those scenarios happened. We learned as we went, and women continued to show up.

Sandy brought her friends, Yseult brought hers, I brought mine. We brought more wine, drank more tea, ordered more pizza, and often we'd be up talking past midnight. I felt a high from the collective transparency of these meetings. We revealed parts of ourselves that were so raw and remote, and reached new levels of understanding that had been hidden in the lies of separateness, hierarchy, and supremacy. It felt radical, like we were having some of the most important conversations we could possibly be having.

About those nights, Sandy told me, "They were such an eye-opener. It made me a lot more open and vulnerable. It was a place where we could shed all our skin. Normally the only place I can do that is with people who look like me. I didn't feel like I was being judged. It made me realize that there are good people out in the world willing to do the work, and willing to understand my perspective and where I'm coming from."

Many women of color would attend the meetings and express that they wished more white people in their life would attend. I felt the same. I wanted every woman I knew to come to listen, to be witnessed, to learn, and to unlearn. I sent out invitations each month to every woman I could think of. My coworkers, my hairdresser, my friends, my cousins. The people from my life who showed up regularly weren't the ones I expected. They weren't always my closest friends, but rather, acquaintances of mine who became friends: clients I only knew through work, coworkers I'd never met before but had heard about the meetups on Slack, or friends of friends. I was especially grateful to the white women I knew who came regularly and was acutely aware of those who came once as a favor to me, and those who did not come at all.

A friend of my husband's, Audrey, a corporate VP at a media company who regularly attended the meetings and became a close friend of mine, told me, "Those early conversations in your living room changed me. The safety and intimacy of that small room allowed me to speak and listen and in a way I'm not sure I'd ever done before. As an immigrant from the Philippines, a country with a long history of Spanish colonization, followed by American imperialism, I suffered from a skewed perception of ethnic and cultural inferiority—otherwise known as colonial mentality—that I had rarely ever explored until those conversations. It catapulted a personal movement for me."

The get-togethers were life changing for me, too. It was powerful to share so vulnerably with each other. At one of the earlier meetings, as the evening was wrapping up, Yseult and I looked at each other, and she said, "We should start a podcast." We saw the power that was happening during our meetings, but it was only available to those who attended. With a podcast, we could bring these dialogues to a wider audience. Within a few weeks, we'd set up a brainstorming session, Yseult had found us a producer, and we booked a recording studio. We were sitting on Yseult's parents' roof in Chelsea when we came up with the name Kinswomen and the concept for the first few episodes.

The monthly sessions between women of color and white women continued to grow. One of our friends, Norma Buster, lent us her company's gorgeous office space to use after hours—she worked for Carrie Goldberg, the renowned women's rights lawyer, and the space, decorated in pink punching bags with views of Manhattan and Brooklyn, was perfect for us.

Yseult and I saw so much potential for *Kinswomen* as a podcast and a place to bring women together. In January 2020, I decided to leave my magazine job and focus on *Kinswomen* full-time, a leap of faith. Then, in March 2020, the pandemic forced us to bring our recording sessions and our meetings to Zoom, but it also allowed women from all over the world to attend the conversations. In June 2020, when it seemed our country was reaching this generation's racial boiling point following the murders of George Floyd, Breonna Taylor, and Ahmaud Arbery, more and more people entered the proverbial chat room.

We found ourselves in a unique position. Where previously, even mention of the work we were doing sometimes made me feel like a pariah to my white peers, suddenly my phone was blowing up with requests to pick our brains about racial issues happening at my friend's jobs, in their families, and with their partners. White people seemed to wake up, en masse, wringing their hands and realizing that our time to act was decades ago.

In response, Yseult and I created classes and worked with companies on their anti-racism journeys. We brought the same kind of radical transparency and (compassionate) accountability that we used in our monthly meetings to groups and corporations. We were no longer just podcasters—we were entrepreneurs and business partners, on top of building our own friendship.

YSEULT P. MUKANTABANA & HANNAH SUMMERHILL

★ ★ ★

Kinswomen is growing into something I envisioned from the first time we brainstormed starting a podcast. I am not surprised or shocked by how it's grown! Mainly because I knew that the conversations that we engaged in were ones that people needed to hear.

Even with more people engaging in these conversations, I don't think things are changing fast enough. This is because there are more BIPOC traumatized and oppressed than the white people "realizing" and finally starting to take action in their lives through advocacy. It's hard for me to dwell on "wins" when there are still so many Black and Brown brothers and fathers in jail for things they shouldn't be incarcerated for, or when there's still a large number of Jewish and Asian people attacked at random in New York. I don't want to focus on making sure white people feel a bit better about themselves when I still feel unsafe in mostly white spaces. I want to focus on changing the situations of people who face discrimination every day. But it all circles back to conversations and fostering relationships. So, let's get started.

TWO

Building Trust: The Foundation of Cross-Racial Dialogues

Bridging the Gaps

No bridges can be built if people aren't willing to see how they're contributing to maintaining the gap, and later, understand that they can become builders to *bridge* the gap. There's no way to fix things if we don't see the problem in the first place.

A big stumbling block to understanding the gaps is when even very well-intentioned white people feel like they are further along than others in their allyship and become upset if their BIPOC friends point out something they're doing that's racist. Because they don't see themselves as being racist, their self-perception makes it that much harder to accept when they've messed up, and calling them in feels like you have to walk on eggshells because they have given themselves an imaginary graduation trophy for being the "Good White Person." I fathom you're challenging the idea that they have of themselves. An analogy to this is if someone has been a leading individual in a field and when they come to find out that there's a new perspective, they get upset because they can't believe that they're not the top dog in the game anymore.

I associate this white fragility to their ego being hurt. I think that these moments are caused by the fact that a lot of white people think that there's a plateau to achieve and that there's a point where they become some type of "expert." The reality is that even I as a Black person am still discovering and learning to recognize and verbalize how white supremacy works in all aspects in my life, so how would any white person ever be an expert? There are no levels to being an ally, but rather there are so many layers to unfold and discover, and I wish white people working on becoming allies were more aware of this fact. The less defensive white people are about the gaps in their understanding, the easier it is to create space and feel closer, especially in friendship.

Sometimes BIPOC shy away from having white friends. One fundamental reason why is because the white people closest to you are often the ones who will demand the most emotional labor. It's like in friendship when a friend takes you for granted because they expect you to have more tolerance to their BS, but why would you? Instead, if you are close, as a white person you should make it a point to be more open and understanding that you will inevitably make a mess, and be willing to listen and fix the mess, out of love. At the very least, apologize and learn to find a way to make it better for next time.

What's challenging about these conversations is that we aren't talking about overt actions like white racists physically harming those who aren't white. It's more about the small comments and people's mindsets—the subtleties that tend to show how aware someone is in these matters. It's like talking to your guy friend about feminism. Obviously, he understands and wants women to be free to live their lives in peace, and he knows that women should wear what they want and have access to education and fair pay. This is more about the subtleties that show up when you try to explain why cat-calling is so problematic. That's the level of awareness and the layers that come into play when we have these conversa-tions about race.

I find myself often wondering, "Am I being over-the-top?" because at times microaggressions feel so "niche" and specific; someone fragile and on the defensive might view me speak-ing up as just coming for the "small stuff," but I know deep down I'm not. The mental and emotional exercise to prepare myself for these kinds of conversations is stress inducing. I do catch myself and try to remember, "This is the gross medicine that will heal us, so fuck it." I just know that for me personally, even if it feels heavy and draining, I owe it to myself to stand fully in my convictions, especially with friends. I've had these conversations with Hannah as well, relating to our friendship and professional collaboration. I want peace, but it's not real peace if someone lives in ignorance to the detriment to an-other's mental and emotional well-being. Also, as a friend, I owe it to be up front about my feelings. Me speaking up is a service to my white friends, so that they are able to do better in other similar situations and have a more positive impact on our relationships.

There are no absolutes as to how to bridge these gaps be-tween women of color and white women. We can lay out the-ories and ideas of how to do it step-by-step, but at the end of the day, white people have to care about restoring their own humanity so that BIPOC and other invisible minorities can live in peace and thrive.

In one of our classes, one of our students was battling with the decision to make her business intentionally anti-racist, and she expressed that she wasn't ready for it. I explained to her that I would not and could not convince her to care for and cre-ate her space with a sense of humanity for those that deserve it. I can't convince a white person to want to be part of this. I can just share my perspective, so that they see clearly. She was moved by my comment but never came back to our course, ashamed probably, that she realized it wasn't something she was willing to intentionally work on.

Bridging the gap between white people and people of color is about reframing what it's really about. It's not so white people become less racist or for white people to love BIPOC; it's to restore the humanity lost in the barbaric history that whiteness has as part of its legacy. To me, it isn't to show we know the most or that we're the best person. Rather, it's deciding that we will not continue to be manipulated by a system that harms BIPOC the way it does.

It means going back in history to understand the harm that was caused and demanding change from our systems and education. The gaps will only be bridged if white people decide to be genuine and not come from a place of self-serving ego/saviorism. To me, it's the same idea as when we say that love alone isn't enough in a relationship, that there's work that has to be done.

Love alone doesn't necessarily build trust, and I understand why women of color have so many reasons not to trust white women, even if we're friends. On a macro level, we have often left out or subordinated women of color in our women's rights efforts, and on an interpersonal level, we wield microaggressions daily. As the Kinswomen, we believe one of the foundations of having constructive conversations on race is building trust. Without trust, there is no transparency, there is no healing, and there is no growth. How do we build trust between women of color and white women, when we're standing on a legacy of abuse, flimsy support, and abandonment?

Just like how I approached Yseult at The Wing, thinking my good intentions would be enough, white women are *never* starting on square one with women of color. There is no fresh page when it comes to interracial interactions, and if we're assuming the privilege of a blank slate, we're being naive. Because we live in a white supremacy culture, we need to be aware that when we enter into an interracial friendship or relationship, we bring the inequity of our systems with us.

Centuries of our violent history echo today, because we do not exist in a vacuum. Context is *vitally* important when we talk about race. White supremacy bets on us forgetting or being completely ignorant of our own history. I distinctly remember learning about the Holocaust in fourth grade—the horrors of it made a huge impression on my young mind. But why are we not teaching students about America's *own* harmful history, like the internment camps that we forced Japanese Americans into during that time? So much has been omitted from our history books, and from our memories. As a child, it was easy to think of the crimes and violence of other countries as being antithetical to American values. Having historical context is the only way to understand where we find ourselves today. In order to bridge the gaps, white people must be intentional in reeducating ourselves and acting from that new lens.

Let's recall the women's suffrage movement. In the late 1800s, the National American Woman Suffrage Association didn't allow Black women to attend their conventions.[8] When women were granted the right to vote in 1920, state laws actively prevented Black women from voting, and they wouldn't have full access until the Voting Rights Act of 1965. In early 2020, much ado was made to celebrate one hundred years of (white) women's suffrage. During this time, I remember seeing a white female artist painting a portrait of the 1920s suffragettes in a subway station, and I asked her if she knew that women's suffrage efforts didn't

---

8   https://www.nps.gov/articles/black-women-and-the-fight-for-voting-rights. htm.

include women of color. She didn't, but after our discussion, the mural continued to go up, day by day, depicting white women in hats with picket signs. Ignoring our legacy of discrimination and only celebrating the progress of white women results in our collective whitewashing of history. We're effectively saying, "Just tell me the good parts and leave out the rest."

I always considered myself a feminist without recognizing how women of color were pushed out or removed from feminist movements and their retellings. These erasures are clear examples of us devaluing the voices, efforts, and needs of women of color. It's as if we as white women gave ourselves the permission to speak for all women, ignoring intersectionality, and doing exactly to women of color what we accuse men of doing to us.

Activist and writer Alice Walker formed her own ideology in response to this: womanism, a movement that centered the experiences of women of color.[9] In her book *In Search of Our Mothers' Gardens*: *Womanist Prose*, she defined a womanist as "A black feminist or feminist of color. Appreciates and prefers women's culture, women's emotional flexibility and women's strength."[10] Womanism creates space for women of color to be seen in their wholeness, and acknowledges the intersection of having to fight both racism and sexism.

Our wage gaps, our political representation, and, as one example, the media flurry over missing white women compared to women of color prove the sad truth that our society sees white women as number one. Media outlets will cover every sordid detail of a missing white woman until answers are uncovered and justice is served, but rarely do we hear about the *hundreds* of missing and murdered Native American women, whose cases

---

9   https://blavity.com/blavity-original/how-alice-walker-created-womanism-the-movement-that-meets-black-women-where-feminism-misses-the-mark?category1=Books.

10   https://bookshop.org/p/books/in-search-of-our-mothers-gardens-womanist-prose-alice-walker/6682921?ean=9780156028646.

are often ignored.[11] Disturbingly, Native women and girls are ten times more likely to be murdered than non-Native women. This gap in coverage and attention reinforces the white-led narratives that only some of us are worthy of life, legacy, and justice, while we continue to brutalize our country's original inhabitants and leave us all more vulnerable to violence with each unsolved and overlooked death of Native and non-white women. (You can learn more and amplify this issue by searching and sharing the hashtag #NoMoreStolenSisters.) Our history books also ignore the contributions of Native women, like lawyer Lyda Conley, the third woman and first Native woman to argue a case before the Supreme Court, in 1909.[12] Or Maria Tallchief, a prima ballerina with the New York City Ballet, who was the first American to dance at the Bolshoi in Moscow[13] and the Paris Opera Ballet.[14] Our lack of both education and empathy for our Native sisters shows us how much more we prize and value white women over women of color. This is not a version of feminism that I want any part of.

I need only look at pictures from my sorority days, or of the bachelorette parties of my twenties and thirties for an example of how the breakdown of trust has divided us. The photos show a sea of white faces. I don't fault my white friends for being white, but acknowledging the whiteness in our spaces is crucial as we aspire toward allyship.

Our photos of friend trips, Greek life, and wedding parties — they usually represent what our lives look like from a racial standpoint. Reflecting upon your own life, is diversity present in your own spaces? Who do you interact with on a daily basis? Who are your peers, and who is in service to you?

---

11 https://www.theguardian.com/us-news/2021/sep/24/native-american-women-missing-murdered-media.

12 https://hellogiggles.com/lifestyle/native-women-learned-history-class/.

13 https://hellogiggles.com/lifestyle/native-women-learned-history-class/.

14 https://www.womenshistory.org/education-resources/biographies/maria-tallchief.

We lose so much in the homogeneity that we enforce. It's comfortable to uphold the norm, and not have to think about race, but our ignorance has an impact. As white women, we both benefit and suffer from "good girl conditioning," which rewards avoiding conflict at all costs in order to maintain harmony. The consequences of our avoidance is that we don't interrupt racism when we see it or hear it, even from our close friends. The larger cost is that we perpetuate racism. I am guilty of this.

Because women value community and belonging, I think most of us want to avoid tension when it comes to challenging group-think. These unspoken social contracts in white friend groups cement a framework over time that doesn't allow outsiders or differing opinions in, and keeps the group homogenous, maintaining an environment where anyone who doesn't conform might be ostracized. At a group dinner with friends several years ago, a member of our party accused another of being "a total Jew" about the check. I felt the nausea and shock from her antisemitic remark (I'm Jewish), but I didn't challenge it. No one else did either. Not only did I feel frozen, I also didn't want to be accused of being uptight or bringing bad vibes to the evening. It was never discussed, so we were all complicit in maintaining the toxic homogeneity.

In our friendship, Yseult and I never want people to look at us from the outside and assume that because we're a Black woman and a white woman doing this work together that we represent some kind of ideal racial harmony. Our relationship takes work every day. It's rewarding, but we're constantly working through the deeper layers: the interpersonal, the societal, the ancestral. Our friendship is built on trust, and we believe each interracial relationship (whether it's business, platonic, or romantic) needs trust first and foremost. Building our foundation of trust has yielded the most beautiful gifts: we can challenge each other without ego, we can express our anger and pain without fear of friendship destruction, we can create space for mess and mis-understanding and growth.

We work within a framework of four pillars that we believe are essential to building trust in cross-racial dialogues: time, transparency, communication, and consistency. In order to build trust and bridge cross-racial gaps, let's get familiar with them.

The Four Foundations

Time

Building trust cannot be rushed. If you consider your close friendships and relationships, those bonds likely didn't form overnight, and it took time for you to trust your partner or your best friend. When it comes to allyship and activism, we need to respect the time that it takes to build trust with individuals and communities. Sometimes, those who are recently awake to social issues think that every person of color should automatically see them as allies, as if BIPOC should assume that they're newly trustable. I remember wondering, "How will people of color know that I'm 'one of the good ones?'" (Cringe.) Instead, trust is built with the building blocks of daily actions over a sustained period of time.

In June 2020, there was a sense of emergency from white people to make immediate changes to our lives, workplaces, and social feeds after the murder of George Floyd. Two years later, as of this writing, there is no more urgency from white people, though the issues remain the same. Had all of us who pledged to be different in 2020 taken daily actions since then, we might be living in a more equitable society today. However, as time went on, the pressure dissipated, and the action fizzled. If we consider ourselves allies, we need to take a long-term view, and if we're not ready to commit to continued action, we should ask ourselves what our values are in the first place, and if we're willing to live in a way that aligns with them.

Time isn't something that white people often give themselves when it comes to this work. The sense of urgency is toxic. It's disturbing when I see someone who has barely dipped a toe in the sea of racial history and knowledge around these issues think they can "save me." As if I exist on the timeline (a racial big bang for BIPOC) of when a white person finally realizes my existence and the racism that I experience. There's grace in accepting that you do not understand everything and will have to unlearn aspects of society that are intrinsically passed down from your ancestors and reinforced by societal dynamics, laws, and institutions.

Also, I speak for myself when I say that I don't even expect or want that. There's no one to save but yourself when you're white. You need time to sit and understand, profoundly, not so you can save someone but to grasp and have confidence in the actions you want to take. This will allow you to understand how you can have a positive impact in your own way, in your own community. No one expects a new swimmer to try out for the Olympics, so why would a white person who is just starting to learn expect to change the whole world? I cannot tell you how hard I roll my eyes internally when I hear a white person tell me during Black History Month, "Hey, I'm here if you need anything." The intention is so kind, but Black History Month should be about taking the opportunity to find events, conversations, books, and so on, to learn from. Because there's nothing I experience in February that I don't already experience all year long. So, if you think you're close enough to extend that attempted "help," you should first take the opportunity to ask yourself, "Hey, it's Black History Month. What's a book I need to read or an event I should attend? How can I educate myself in a meaningful way to take the burden off others?" That's ultimately a better use of time and offers a more productive viewpoint that anti-racism work is an ongoing, long-term activity.

Transparency

As white people, there's no guarantee of comfort when it comes to talking about race. To be transparent, I am never truly comfortable, and I often feel insecure, unsure, and anxious when it comes to these dialogues. When we first started hosting the living room sessions, white women who would attend for the first time would often sit in silence, afraid of saying something wrong, just as I did when I attended the event where I first met Yseult. Being open about the tension allows it to be discussed and learned from. There's power in vulnerably accepting that there is a lot we don't know and that we will mess up.

I've messed up many times. Even when we're doing our best, we have to admit that we're not experts and that there will be lots of growing pains. Learning in public is a strength, because the transparency allows others to be brave, too.

Centering transparency in this work is admitting where we are. Another toxic idea is that because you're in this space of activism, you're supposed to be a superexpert. It's not written anywhere that that's what anyone is expecting you to be. Do the work consistently and be open to learning and unlearning.

Transparency also means admitting and coming clean about when you mess up. It reminds me of when I realized I needed to quit drinking. After I made my decision and I felt like my life was getting back on track, I had an urge to address my closest friends and family about how I had failed them while I struggled with alcohol. I wanted to address the hurt I had caused so that I could build good and healthy relationships. Mainly, I wanted those I loved the most to understand that I was accountable for the harm I'd caused, and I really meant to make things better.

I think white people need to have the same attitude: come to peace with what you have participated in and how you've contributed to harm on an interpersonal level with your friends of color or your Jewish friends—acknowledge the weird and cringey racist jokes. Or, on a corporate level, own up to how you have let down your employees of color or any other marginalized communities present. Transparency is the only way to build a healthy and genuine path to becoming a real ally, because you have to acknowledge reality before you can grow and do better.

Communication

In order to build strong trust and relationships in cross-racial (or any) settings, we need to communicate clearly and listen with intention. Sometimes I feel confident in sharing my views, and sometimes I feel like my throat is constricted with fear of getting it wrong. And sometimes, I have to hear hard truths, like when Yseult shares that something I've said was problematic. I have to accept the impact without centering my intentions and feelings or blaming the person who shared the incident with me instead of looking critically at my actions. The reality is that we will fumble in uncomfortable conversations, but communication is the goal, not perfection.

When others are speaking about their identity and experiences, listen and validate. If I told my husband, for example, that something he experienced as racism wasn't actually what happened, it'd be disrespectful and invalidating. As a white person,

I do not get to decide what is racism and what is not. I need to be mindful of my words and the space I take up in a cross-racial conversation and let those who are the experts lead. However, we can't let our discomfort keep us silent or unwilling to engage.

I personally believe that any meaningful work must start from within when we want it to be real. Communication has to begin with yourself, friends, and local communities. There's this flawed idea that white people need to insert themselves into BIPOC communities and spaces in order to learn how to be anti-racist, or that bringing BIPOC into white spaces is the solution to solving racism. But really, there are enough books, lectures, and recorded events from a variety of BIPOC that can be a good starting place for learning. It's also important to note that just because someone is a BIPOC person that they don't necessarily have the tools, answers, and bandwidth to teach white people. It can be retraumatizing when a BIPOC person has to hear how white people have messed up and harmed fellow BIPOC. It's also not necessary to hear trauma stories—events that minorities and marginalized communities experience at the hands of white supremacy and white people.

I think we have to normalize talking about racism with our own white friends. I understand why friends shy away from these conversations, because it's natural to want to focus on commonalities instead of what sets us apart and might potentially cause awkwardness. I think that's why interracial relationships often overlook or purposefully leave out talking about what it's like for the person of color in that dynamic. That being said, I know through my friends' experiences and my own that not having these conversations ultimately *does* create distance. And as the Black person, it's important to me to know if my friend has problematic or racist beliefs.

Talking about race should be as natural as other topics that real friends talk about. One example is if you're friends with a

Black person who's going to give birth, you could be checking on how your friend feels and be open to hearing the hurdles and dangers they may be facing giving birth in the US. Real friendship is more than wanting to dress up in your friend's cultural clothing, or eating the amazing food that's authentic to their culture. Friendship should cover the good and bad. The responsibility of the white friend is to be proactive in knowing and being open to chatting about what your friend experiences in everyday life.

The biggest hurdle to communication that I've experienced, and I imagine is common for BIPOC to have had to experience at some point, is the defensiveness that comes up from white fragility. I've learned to recognize when I've reached my threshold, and take the actions necessary to protect myself, often removing myself from the conversation. The most beautiful thing we can offer our friends is boundaries. As a Black woman, I need them to feel safe in my relationships. My boundaries are knowing when to step away, breathe, pray, and compose myself, accepting that I do not have to be the teacher and expert on all things racism. I remind myself that I get to exist in spaces where my humanity and identity isn't a resource for someone else. I have learned how to say no and not be emotionally drained by the by-product of white fragility and white shame, because I don't have the magic to change that in people—they do.

Even though it's often uncomfortable and emotional work to learn how to communicate with friends, it's completely worth it, for yourself and for the peace it brings your friendships. The way I have personally normalized including my whole identity with my white friends is that I plan dinners where we dish about life. We each bring all aspects of our lives and organically, if it makes sense and feels right, I'll bring up things that are related to me being a queer Black woman. At this point, it's not something I consciously have to think about with my close friends.

With new people that I don't know, I test the waters just so I know what the temperature is like.

Friendships are chosen families and the opportunity to be with people who share our same values. White friends: be cool and kind, don't make this about you, decenter from the discomfort, and if your friends take the chance to open up, hold space to listen in down times and also make sure to uplift and rejoice when something good is happening. I just want people to understand that BIPOC exist in more than one reality, and the good things have to be celebrated; being a good friend is recognizing that. At the end of the day, what's most important is being a decent human, not a perfect one. White people have to remember that it takes work on their end as much as it takes us patience on ours to maintain the relationship.

Consistency

Going to one march or reading one book on anti-racism and expecting radical internal or external change is like brushing your teeth once and thinking you never have to again. When we first started hosting the living room sessions, sometimes we would only have four people attend. The small showing could have made me want to scrap the series altogether, worried that people would stop coming entirely, but after over a year of meetings, the participation increased, and we never had to worry about attendance. Our group never would have found the community and healing that it did if I was deterred by others' lack of enthusiasm in the beginning. I trusted that eventually people would come around if I continued to show up and offer the space.

Allyship work requires steadiness and reliability to be effective. If we want to bridge gaps between white people and people of color, there will be no trust if we do not continue to make our values clear and live by them on a regular basis. It may sound forced, but each day I challenge myself to take action on my values. If allyship is new for us, we have to be super conscious to make it a habit.

Consistency isn't foreign to whiteness, but it seems forgotten when we are talking about racial and human injustices. There's an initial will to want to "help," but all too soon the urgency subsides and the action fades. I am convinced white people know how to be consistent in their allyship. I have seen with my own two eyes that it's possible for white people to be supportive and amazing advocates for things they care about.

Take the veganism movement for instance. A whole culture and industry have been created around it: restaurants, support groups, farms, and nonprofit organizations meant to fight against the killing of animals. I mean, I low-key feel envious of the cows and chickens that receive such consistent support and advocacy. And as a result, there has been real progress made to protect and save these poor animals from being mistreated. When someone who takes our course asks me how to be an ally, I tell them to be like their vegan friends. Be *that* committed and show as much consistency and compassion as die-hard vegans have for animals—just imagine what that would look like. We would be alright! We'd have more aware restaurants and workplaces and have better work environments for BIPOC and minorities of all kinds. People would feel comfortable to have tough conversations and demand change because they would feel seen and understood. We would even have less BIPOC in prisons, and schools wouldn't be segregated. I would love to see communities come together and dedicate this much time and resources to help solve the problem of racism.

I think the best way to show up, and the easiest way to stay consistent, is to start where we are familiar. If you love art, find a space that centers conversation with diverse artists. Or if you're into medicine, investigate what BIPOC peers in medicine are discussing. Be active, because advocacy is needed everywhere, and because one person cannot speak on everything. Wherever your spheres of interest and influence are, that's where your voice is needed the most.

These four pillars of time, transparency, communication, and consistency are the key building blocks to keep in mind within your interracial relationships.

The Pillars in Practice

I believe that these pillars should be regarded as a foundation of values to anchor you in being part of change. You should look at them as guidelines to start genuine dialogues. Putting these pillars into action can be challenging, so it's important to have a road map of what it looks like in practice, know where you are on your journey, and the tools you have.

For me, it's important to see that my white friends are engaging in their own way, not just when something horrible happens (which is every day). These pillars can help us normalize caring and make it an organic thing in our lives. This doesn't have to be done in any specific way, and it doesn't have to be visible to me all the time. For me, it means friends talking about a book they are reading by a BIPOC author or sharing about a new BIPOC artist they discovered they think I might like. These pillars, like everything I share, are meant to move away from the status quo that robs people from connecting with the world we share. It's a real blessing to be connected to the world that surrounds us in a way that feels real and isn't based on the structure that whiteness is right, and the rest isn't.

These pillars are fundamental but not exclusive; they should be added to and curated based on who the individual is. And it's okay to admit that you don't always have the same energy to contribute, and life happens. The idea is that white people who claim to care and want to participate in change should find a sustainable way to do so. The responsibility should be greater for those who have the most privilege. Caring about the BIPOC community needs to become the air you breathe and the food you consume, as "natural" to the fabric of life as the racism I experience every day. I imagine that some people reading this might think this is an intense view, but again, it's not as intense as the racism I experience every day. The ask here is to care and to take action toward that care.

People who want to become allies need to exercise this with daily action and awareness. If something comes up, notice it, address it and find a place to express it, and do something about it. If you're a parent with children, allyship means trying to figure out if their school is addressing diversity, and making sure that your children are aware of what racism looks like, so they can come to you and tell you if they see this kind of behavior from a teacher or other adult. I experienced racism as soon as I entered school for the first time. All these daily practices translate to creating an awareness, because hate thrives in silence and feeds off ignorance.

In the work that we do with *Kinswomen*, being intentional about these pillars comes up in a variety of ways. We do a lot of work with different groups, and often it's mostly white people who want to learn how to put to practice these pillars in their lives. It doesn't bother me that it's mostly white people— it would be weird if it was mostly BIPOC; white people really are the ones that need to be doing intentional and meaningful work. I secretly applaud them but tend to hold back on vocalizing it, because I know a few are there—consciously or unconsciously—to get a "Good White Person" badge, and I don't have any to hand out.

Sometimes we have a diverse group, and that's when weird things can happen. The white women assume that the few BIPOC in the room are there to teach them, or at least indirectly, they expect them to guide. That's when I like to remind the white people in the room that this initiative must be on them. There's this intrinsic belief that BIPOC have the keys and solutions for all the harm that white supremacy has caused; the truth is that most of us must recognize it and try to make sense of it, but the answer isn't something we have all set and ready to hand out.

Honestly, it's easy to spot when someone isn't doing this work for the right reasons and hasn't taken time to answer their "why?" And the answer should always be about oneself. A big aspect of this work is accepting that you won't be able to do it alone. And finding resources and tools with like-minded people is a great way to start.

These pillars are easy to read and understand, but as with everything, it comes down to applying them. I think we have fallen into a habit of looking for simple and fast solutions, but nothing changes overnight just because you know the concepts. Kind of like how you can buy a cookbook to start learning how to cook, but being a chef takes time and application.

THREE
The Spectrum of Racism

The Myth of Racist "Over There"

If I were asked several years ago if I was racist, I would most likely have gotten angry, defensive, and insisted that I was color-blind. But I grew up living in a white supremacist culture in which racism infects everything, including my understanding of the world. If you flinched when I said "white supremacist culture" because it sounds radical, overdramatic, or because you disagree, let me explain.

White supremacy means that the further away one is from whiteness, the less privileges they have. Whiteness in our country literally reigns *supreme*. So many of our laws, social norms, and precedents have been created by and to serve white people while causing harm to people of color, which has been the case since this land was colonized by the arrival of white settlers. While some might argue that this part of our history happened a long time ago, our culture is still deeply white-centered, and the majority of those who exist outside of whiteness still suffer from wealth, health, education, and opportunity gaps based on the laws, policies, and collective belief systems of white people. In white supremacy, white, able-bodied, cisgender, heterosexual, male and Christian bodies make up the epicenter of our society's privilege.

It is impossible to avoid absorbing the messages of white superiority that our culture propagates, since it's embedded in all of our media, education, and institutions. But we each have a responsibility in adulthood to question and dismantle the brain- and whitewashing that we may not have had awareness of for so many years.

I think that most of us, as white people, would never consider ourselves to be racist. When we imagine racism, we picture extreme acts, like white hoods burning crosses, or neo-Nazis, or white people using the N-word. These examples make any implication of our own racist behavior feel like the worst possible accusation. I can understand wanting to distance ourselves from it, but denying our own internalized racism shuts down any conversation about these issues, so we never get to the acknowledgment, apologies, or repair.

Overtly racist people, like those who participate in the examples above, are abhorrent, but they are in the minority. Most of us act on the spectrum of racism—and all of it is harmful. While we may not be waving swastikas, we're still harboring and acting on implicit bias and ignorance, and being the ones with the most privilege and in most positions of power, our behavior impacts the lives of people of color every day.

If you take the time to listen to BIPOC, and learning from what Yseult has shared with me, the worst behavior comes from well-meaning, and often, liberal white friends, colleagues, relatives. That means, for most of us, that we need to reverse the direction of our finger-pointing.

The "over there" attitude is common whenever we don't want to be associated with what looks bad or feels wrong. We point to others to dissociate from our own behavior and actions, which deflects from real accountability. I think it's a natural and impulsive thing to do. When it comes to racism, this is a common stance that's taken. But it's like pointing a finger at a raging forest fire when your own home is burning. White people conveniently want to overlook their own mess and problematic viewpoints. There's a lot of energy that's spent calling people out within white communities and not enough calling each other in or identifying racism in their own behavior.

One of the reasons why it's so hard for white people to see themselves as being harmful is because the entire culture has been built in their image. And anywhere whiteness has been a default, the narrative will naturally be white-centered, and it's always problematic. It makes sense that because you see the world through your experiences, and if yours has always been white, well, it seems "normal" if everything is filtered through this whiteness.

An example that I like to give is how Jesus is commonly portrayed as a white man with straight hair and blue eyes in almost all the book and movie depictions. This is even though historically Jesus was a Middle Eastern Jew, and he would have most likely had olive skin, brown curly hair, and brown eyes. There's a systemic disconnect between these two portrayals because these stories are produced and written by white people that have been raised and socialized in a world that tells them that Jesus was a white man.

Some might say that not all movies are supposed to be historically accurate, but if that's the case, why is the default always whiteness? And what is the message we're sending if we are whitewashing parts of history? Also, it's important to remember that during colonization and slavery, religion was a powerful tool used to make Indigenous people obey the colonizers.

The "over there" mentality also comes up in our workshops

when we have the chance to talk to people from all over the world. Since we operate with America as a default—because of where our business is physically located and because most of our clients are Americans—I find myself having to remind our students that racism isn't just something that the US must deal with. Anywhere where whiteness is the ruling hand, you'll have white supremacy as a default in the nation and people. It presents itself differently, obviously, in different countries, because the history isn't the same.

In Canada for example, there wasn't a mass importation of enslaved people from Africa like there was in the US, so while racism is still very present for Black Canadians, the historical context is different from the US. But they do have a horrid and barbaric history of mistreatment of Indigenous peoples. The mostly free healthcare system and so many "sorry"s from Canadians doesn't diminish that they, too, have done some horrible things, and minorities and First Nations people still experience systematic and oppressive treatment from the Canadian government. When we have Canadians in the room, I make it a point to remind them that it's not just their cousins in the US—they, too, have an ongoing issue and history to investigate.

It's flawed to think that white supremacy shows up the same today as it did in the past. But just because it doesn't look and sound the same doesn't mean that the same ideologies aren't at hand. Owning up to the racist history would give more space for healthy and constructive conversation. Otherwise, we're stuck with fragile white folks that need a belly rub every time they feel like they have done something slightly positive. America in comparison to Canada seems like "the racist down there," but as with individuals, there is no free pass that comes from comparison.

Everyone treats white supremacy like a hot potato that they

want to throw at someone else to feel a little better. I think all white nations and people need to embrace that the heat they feel won't go away until it's acknowledged and new systems are put into place for equality. It might not be your fault that all of these things happened and you may not have direct power to make things better, but it's your responsibility as a white person and potential ally to take on the heat and work to have a positive impact.

"Subtle" Racism

When Yseult and I are together in public, working or sharing a meal, I've noticed a pattern. Wherever we go, white women regularly approach her, bashfully or aggressively, like she's a celebrity. They usually say, "I *love* your outfit," or "I just wanted to let you know that you're so *pretty.*"

Something about these interactions always felt off to me, but it took a while for me to articulate why. I thought about it: Why would these women consistently feel comfortable interrupting our conversations? Why does their gushing seem so conditional, like they want something from Yseult, or like they're testing her? Have I ever done this?

After witnessing one exchange, I said to Yseult, "Is it weird? All of these white women complimenting you all the time?" It felt like they were trying to prove how *not* racist they were by letting Yseult know they were "totally cool" with her in the space, letting her know that she had their approval, but also seeking hers as a way to alleviate their guilt. I could only recognize it because I could see myself in them. Several years ago, I might have had the same impulse.

Yeah—racism, and its by-products, has a funny way of showing itself. Those women probably aren't used to seeing a Black woman in a predominantly white space and have no idea how to react to it. They need to prove that "they aren't like the other ones." Meanwhile, all I want is to grab my coffee or have my meeting in peace.

I think it's like when you're on a first date, and you feel so awkward that you decide to go on a tangent about the weather. You feel like you have to say something, otherwise your date will think that the silence is weird. Personally, I like deafening, awkward silences—it means you might not know what to say, but you don't want to leave the conversation either. Silence requires vulnerability. But these women feel the need to make their presence known.

Instead of filling the void with boring weather talk—which I would prefer, to be honest—these white women often decide that the best way to handle their discomfort is to compliment me. I'm not mad about it. It just feels objectifying. It's not really about my outfit of the day, it's more to drown out the awkwardness of the situation they are in. It's definitely funny and entertaining, too. I always wonder if they know what I'm seeing or if they can recognize that they aren't completely comfortable. There's no real logical reason for their discomfort either. I haven't said anything, and probably haven't even noticed them.

I also know and recognize that part of the reason why they come up to me is because they must see something in me that they want to claim. My likeness elevates their presence around me and maybe soothes their guilt if I receive them well. They take into account my body or the fashion I wear, because it leads them to classify me based on my financial status and gauge if we are "in" together or not. The gag is that *all* my shit is cheap. Maybe I am also just the right shade of Black to make them feel like I'm approachable. I've had people remark to me that I was really pretty and had "very pleasing features for a Black girl." Or that I must be mixed, which for them meant mixed with Black and white—whiteness as the lead mixer to make BIPOC beautiful within the white standard. Absurd! Imagine if I walked up to a white person and said all that! Everyone would look at me with confusion, like I had lost my common sense of decency. These interactions, no matter how intellectualized they have become to me, never make sense and will always rob me of my energy.

When I was younger, I would casually entertain these interactions, but now, early in my thirties, I keep a straight face and whisper to myself, "I will not feed your feel-good quota for the day, Brianna." I never want to seem rude, because I am my mother's child, but I just don't have it in me to smile and prance to make white people more comfortable. It feels like low-vibration energy.

It's nothing at all like when I am complimented by a "sister" from another mister. Getting praise from Black women is the closest I get to feeling like I've been graced by the moon herself, like someone just handed me a warm glass of milk and freshly made chocolate chip cookies. In all Black women, I see a little of my grandmother, mother, and aunts, and I feel pulled in by the warm arms of the universe. I love these interactions with other Black women because, I think secretly, we give each other hype to remind us of who we are and that whatever mental and emotional anguish we're experiencing, we are seen by our own and given a space to feel whole again. I feel an instant restoration to my humanity.

It's fascinating to hear Yseult's perspective of this, and how she can pretty much predict white women's reactions to her clothes and her "approachable Blackness." I'm embarrassed by how easily WOC[15] can see right through our bullshit. I don't think most white people would consider these compliments a

---

15   WOC = woman/women of color.

form of racism, but fetishizing and tokenizing Black people is a form of othering, and it feels like a form of white saviorism to expect Black people to be grateful when we "grant" them our approval.

During one of our living room sessions, a Black woman who worked on a team of white people shared a similar story to what Yseult has experienced, and it illustrates what happens on the other side of this "praise":

"My bosses always say to me, 'Oh, Christine,[16] you're so gorgeous. You're a model,' as if that's enough for me to forget that I haven't been promoted in five years, even though I consistently get incredible evaluations, and white women with less experience get promoted above me."

I think sometimes we believe it's enough that we show surface-level approval to the people of color in our space. Like: "Compliment given! My work is done and I'm not a racist." Compliments do not solve racism, though. Instead, we should be thinking about the structural improvements we can make, like granting the overdue promotions and raises that our colleagues of color deserve and changing a work culture that breeds microaggressions and only celebrates Blackness on MLK Day.

In the past, if a friend or coworker of color had shared with me a racist incident that they experienced, like getting cut in front of in line by a white person, or asked where they were "really" from, I might have tried to convince them the slight wasn't racial, in an effort to make them feel better. That impulse, however, invalidates what they experienced—as someone who knows from past experiences that it *was* racial, even if I as a white person wasn't conscious of it. I think that dehumanizing someone by trying to convince them that they're unable to decipher their own interactions with racism is racist in itself. When our friends or col-

---

16   Name has been changed.

leagues share their experiences of the world with us, whether it's joy or pain, we can only build trust by being a validating place for them to vent or gush or cry, instead of minimizing the moment. And it's okay not to know exactly what your friend might need. We can always ask.

When we engage in anti-racism work, it's crucial that we focus on impact over intention. Most of us don't *intend* to be racist, but we may be having a harmful impact on people of color. Becoming aware of the unconscious power dynamics we create and the danger that exists around our whiteness, even if don't intend to participate in this kind of harm, is necessary.

Imagining a line where we exist on either the "racist" or "not racist" side is a way we deny the impact of our actions. We'll always declare ourselves on the side of *not*.

But bias is normal, even though it can be difficult to admit. Only when we reject the "either/or" lie and come to terms with the impact of our bias can we have honest conversations about racism.

As white people, we must make the subconscious *conscious* when it comes to our conditioned racist thinking, because being unaware is not an excuse. Taking the time to look at the ugly parts of ourselves is an exercise that's necessary for us as white aspiring allies.

It's in seemingly minor, everyday interactions that our racial hierarchies are revealed.

I was recently stopped on the street in Paris by a woman asking for directions. When I'm in big cities, especially while traveling abroad, I'm cautious when being approached by strangers. The woman who stopped me was unthreatening—she was pushing a stroller—but I noticed that my guard was up. She had dark hair and olive skin, and upon walking away, I wondered, *If she'd had blond hair, or was American, would my guard have been up as much?* Inquiry into the ways in which I believe I'm protecting myself based on others' physical appearances isn't a fun exercise—it brings up feelings of shame, denial, and guilt—but it's important that I question my conditioning *and* consider the impact it has on those I'm projecting it onto.

Our deeply ingrained, or implicit,[17] bias can cause emotional and physical harm to the people of color around us. We have to take responsibility for not just our own bias but also how we interact within a collectively biased society.

Once, in the car with my husband, I started an argument—probably over something trivial. He pulled into our apartment building's parking lot so that he wasn't trying to placate me while driving. "You're not seeing your privilege right now at being able to get angry in public at me, whereas I can't do that. If people were to see us, they might see an angry Black man yelling at a white woman, get scared, and call the police. I'm not *allowed* to express those emotions." Even though I was heated, I had to acknowledge that he was right, and that even the very mundane reality of arguing with a partner carries potentially harmful implications if it's a cross-racial interaction. I should have been aware of how our fighting would be perceived in a white supremacy.

We've all absorbed racial and ableist stereotypes that have embedded themselves so deeply that we don't notice we have them. These reflexes might surface when we drive through a Black neighborhood, or when we go to an Asian spa, or see someone who's in a wheelchair. Whether we realize it or not, we make judgments about people's abilities, intelligence, profession, social status, or perceived threat to us. The point is not to feel shame about these feelings, but to bring awareness to them so we can begin to question them.

---

17. Implicit bias: "when we have attitudes towards people or associate stereotypes with them without our conscious knowledge." https://perception.org/research/implicit-bias/

The myth of this duality of being racist or not allows us to opt out of doing anti-racism work and taking responsibility. If most people consider themselves "not racist," then there is nothing to do but point fingers at those who are. Instead of thinking, "I'm better than my neighbor, because I didn't vote for [insert polarizing politician here]," be honest about your own biases and their impact, and avoid the hierarchical social organizing that white supremacy propagates.

I think that the hardest part of dealing with these by-products of racism is having to bring it up. Because it's not "obvious harm," it's more difficult to deal with because white people truly believe that they are doing something nice.

Most white people will get defensive if I point something out and will be so focused on making sure I don't think that they are racists that they miss what I'm trying to communicate about their behavior. In situations that require calling in a white person close to me, I have had to deal with it in such a specific way. The time and energy that I am willing to grant in this dynamic is only when I'm really close to the person, and it's because I care about them changing or because I was really hurt. The reason why I have to be selective is because the process is draining and retraumatizing in many ways. It's a boundary that I have had to lay out for my own mental well-being. When a white person reacts defensively, we enter the phases below:

Phase one is "Mothering": I have to spend a considerable amount of time making sure they know that I think they're nice people, and that I still care about them. This is something that white people expect from BIPOC and at times will even use against us. If I don't preface my conversations with these platitudes, I typically receive defensive comments like "I feel like I can't say or do anything right" or "I don't feel like I have space to grow and learn."

Phase two is "The Breakdown": This is the most exhausting part, personally, because I have to peel back the onion of why what they said or did is racist and problematic. This means I have to put my whole feelings aside to explain something that made me feel emotional, often without the time to heal or process the moment. It's challenging because sometimes the emotion I'm processing is betrayal, because this person is my friend or significant other and they have done something harmful to me. At times, I wonder how I found myself in this situation and put unrealistic expectations on myself as to how I could have avoided the situation.

Phase three is "The Tears": There's a period in which the person realizes they have messed up or feels ashamed of their behavior, and the idea of them having said or done something that can be categorized as racist translates into tears. It also can translate into the form of defensiveness and combativeness. This is when I just want to run away and not deal with it, because tears come off as a way to shut down the conversation. I've been in a situation where someone said, "How can you continue to talk about this? Don't you see I'm crying?" It's not supposed to be a cue to ending the conversation, especially if I'm making space to "fix" it or to explain how I feel. The white women's tears in this interaction are tools to shut it down and just make you feel like the bad person in a dynamic where you have been hurt. I've been in situations where white women cry not because it's become a shouting match, but because of their anxiety over where they know the conversation is going.

Phase four, "Cool Down": This is not always immediate—it depends on the person, and if I'm still there. But sometimes there is a space for conversation and apologies about the situation. It feels late and repetitive—it's not the first time and won't be the last. I also have to hope that it means that the next

time this conversation comes up they're more aware and can react better, but that's often not the case from my experience.

I write these phases with light humor only because it's what I've experienced time and time again. This is meant to show why these conversations are not on a level playing field. I'm faced with attitude because white people want to feel like they are the "good ones," and that they understand. There's no time to actually accept that they don't. I've experienced moments where anger and resentment build up with friends, as if I created these dynamics and personally made these things happen. The nature of my personality also doesn't help because I cannot just let it go. I feel a pile of weight sitting on my chest if my white friend is completely unaware of my hurt. No, we are going to sit in this discomfort together if we are going to be friends. Let's talk about it and move forward together. Or not, and if needed, we can take separate paths.

I understand why some of my Black friends say they can't be around white people. I've witnessed white people shocked and utterly horrified that someone wouldn't want to befriend them because they're white. But it's rare for them to try to understand why someone would feel like that. It's a burden to know how to address these moments, and honestly, it's not like anyone teaches us how to. So not everyone wants to, not because they inherently hate white people but rather as a way to cope and shield themselves from the mental and emotional anguish of these difficult moments. It hurts so much more when you experience something racist when the person is close. It feels like a bigger betrayal, often not because of the harm caused, but because of their reaction to realizing they have said something racist and the aftermath.

As a Black woman in these situations, I feel like I am left to pick myself back up. It adds to all the other things you're left to pick yourself up from. I don't have any easy answers for

how Black women can protect themselves. But I will say from my experience that it's essential to find a space where there's community that looks like you. I have found that it helps me recharge and exist in a space that centers my Blackness, without having to think about it. I experience this whenever I'm home in Rwanda.

We have to let go of the idea that BIPOC have to be the bigger people in our friendships and interactions with white people. White people need to understand that individually they have an impact on people and it's a personal responsibility of theirs to make sure they don't add to the burden. This doesn't mean they have to have all the answers and single-handedly fix racism. But rather when something comes up and a friend says it hurts, to just lick the wound and be there as a friend with loving and comforting words.

In a professional setting, making sure there's space for BIPOC and allies to speak up is one way of showing support. Not just to say a door is open, but more importantly, to initiate a space of conversation, workshops, and interactions that show you actually want to do the work. It's like in intimate relationships—when there are issues within a couple and a partner says, "I'm here to talk." What goes so much further is initiation, like, "Hey, let's take this intimacy course together, or let's start therapy and address this together." Saying that the "door is open" isn't enough—it's about creating a safe space to engage and making actionable change as a result of those dialogues.

No Excuses for Exclusion

There's been so much talk about inclusion in recent years. The word is used frequently by us as white people as an antidotal balm to all of our racial transgressions. But before we discuss inclusion,

can we be honest about who we've been excluding, why, and the repercussions of that exclusion?

It took years for me to notice who was being excluded from my workplaces. While there were people of color in my previous corporate jobs, I didn't consider why there were so few. Most of the people I worked alongside during my twelve years in magazines were (visibly) white, able-bodied, cisgender, and college educated, and many seemed to come from generational wealth. If they were covering or code-switching their identities to fit into the norm, I wasn't aware. In fact, I was mostly concerned with how *I*, as an able-bodied cisgender white woman, *didn't* fit into the magazine world. I often didn't feel tall, thin, or wealthy enough compared to the ideal that the industry prized. One job demanded that we, as sales reps, buy designer clothing and bags, which I couldn't afford in addition to New York rent, even with my six-figure salary and lack of student loans. The message was that to have a "dream-job," six-figure opportunity, you had to already be rich.

For years, I was so focused on my own perceived lack of privilege that I wasn't thinking about what the environment was like for those who existed even further from privilege's nucleus. As part of the majority, I was naive to what employees of color, disabled employees, or those from low-income communities had to endure, what kept them at the job or didn't, and who we were actively (but "unintentionally") excluding from our workplace. I personally didn't think I was excluding anyone when I, after being promoted, was tasked with hiring an assistant, nor did I question why the assistants that I interviewed or hired were women who looked just like me. Our culture was literally exclusive, like many workplaces are. Because it's where we spend a lot of our time and is the source of our livelihoods, recognizing how this exclusion harms BIPOC and marginalized communities is vital to understanding the systemic nature of white supremacy and our responsibility to change it.

Homogenous workplaces are toxic for everyone. A lack of diversity from whiteness at an organization, for example, enforces a norm that asks anyone outside of it to contort to that norm, instead of allowing their differences to enrich it. Such an environment doesn't usually bode well for the longevity of those who identify outside of whiteness, to which conforming can be mentally exhausting and harmful. From a business standpoint, that leads to low retention of people of color, and a less welcoming environment for new or remaining minority employees, or those from marginalized communities. A homogenous workplace flattens a company's marketing efforts and messaging by only speaking from a singular voice and appealing to a particular demographic. From a structural lens, when people of color are excluded from workplaces, they miss out on the networking opportunities, salaries, and benefits that could help close the wage and health gaps. So much is lost when the majority rules.

Diversity alone will not make our organizations better. We need inquiry into what we desire to be diverse *from*, and that requires being honest about "defaults" and norms within the organization. From my observations in work spaces, often the expectation is that once people of color have been hired, the company can check its diversity box, fully expecting their new employees to feel grateful and assimilate to the white work culture. But diversity isn't synonymous with inclusion and equity.

I've heard many white employees across industries huff about their efforts to diversify backfiring. "We tried that and it didn't work," is a common sentiment from those in positions of power, who seem surprised when their new employees of color don't conform to workplace culture, fit in quietly, express gratitude—or when they criticize the organization publicly after they leave.

Rarely does the white majority at an organization question how they've created a hostile environment for people of color.

When I'd hear my colleagues express attitudes like this, I'd freeze, because I didn't know how to reconcile their racist words with my often positive feelings toward them. I didn't have the education or vocabulary to articulate in the moment *why* what they said was so problematic.

That's been a major learning curve in my allyship journey—being able to better and more quickly recognize racism and why it's harmful. Before, I just knew that it felt wrong, and I would freeze in finding the words to share why. "Noticing" racism is not enough, though. The hardest part is sharing that "why" with someone in a way where they hear it, and not delivering it in a way where I sound patronizing or accusatory, as well as taking responsibility for problematic behavior I may be perpetuating or contributing to. We'll bring you through how to navigate interactions like these in an upcoming chapter.

Having conversations about race in a professional setting is not easy, but if a company truly wants to create a safe and equitable workplace, here are some questions that must be asked and answered honestly:

- Who is the "default" employee or manager?

- What are the hiring processes, and what are the biases within them?

- Who makes the most at the company, and who makes the least? Is there salary parity among different groups?

- Do BIPOC, queer, trans, or disabled employees see examples of people who look like them at the top?

- Will those employees have to "code-switch" at work? I.e. whitewash or erase parts of themselves to fit into the environment?

- Do managers acknowledge what's happening in the news and culture, and how that could be affecting certain communities more so than others?

- Is the company only hiring candidates from four-year universities or from employee recommendations? What's preventing the company from expanding their scope to source from low-income communities, community colleges, or those with no degree at all?

- Is the company investing in regular anti-racism training?

- Are there employee resource groups available to support minority and/or marginalized communities at work?

- Is the culture one where people feel safe bringing their full selves to work, and does it foster open communication and discourse on identity, gender, access, and racism?

Not considering these things in the workplace might not be intentional, but that doesn't mean the oversight has a neutral impact on employees of color.

I have observed that when it comes to exclusion of BIPOC, it can be broken into two different parts—societal and interpersonal. I feel that everyone can relate to the interpersonal one—one-on-one relationships with our friends, families, and partners. The societal refers to where you work, your clubs or other organizations, your hobbies, even the gym where you work out. As a BIPOC, everywhere you go requires you to be self-aware in relation to a chosen space.

White people might notice they're participating in interpersonal exclusion when they realize they're surrounded by mostly white people, even though there are many faces that represent the real world we all share and live in. My take is that if you have managed to exclude all people that don't look like you in your life, consciously or unconsciously (because I do believe a lot of white people do it without really realizing it), it's kind of robbing yourself of understanding the world we live in.

One day I was invited to a very American and white home somewhere deep in Pennsylvania. The outside entrance had big white columns like you'd see in Texas or in the Southern states, an aesthetic that makes me think about plantations. The columns and vibes alone were an amuse-bouche for the cringey situation that I knew I was about to experience. I mean, in situations when I know I'm about to step into a very white and potentially weird space, I find humor in knowing that at least I'll have a story to share.

I predicted I'd probably be the only Black person there. These moments for me feel like a real social experiment. I know that someone at some point will say something worth a hard side-eye. When I enter these spaces, it's like walking into a new room on a video game. Everyone there was nice and polite. I felt observed, but nothing aggressive.

At some point, in the corner of the room I saw a Black guy, and I got a little happy, ready to high-five this stranger, thinking he must have felt how odd and funny everyone there was. I took my weird self over to him and said hi. He was super polite and welcoming, but I didn't feel the "Oh, sis" vibe, so I felt alone again. He pressed me with some pretty personal questions: "Where are you from?" "Who did you come with?" I just needed him out of my pocket, so I ended our conversation abruptly, lying that I had to pee, and walked away, but not before he told me he's known this family for a long time and they've basically adopted him. That was followed by a big, shared laugh between him and a white guy I hadn't noticed next to him. I gulped my drink hard and just walked away.

Looking back, this was a very "sunken place" moment, a term coined by the movie *Get Out*, where the Black characters are taken to homes of white people who steal the life force from their bodies to stay young and healthy. I went to find my date, who was hanging out with a bunch of his friends. They were all nice and pretty and inviting, especially the girl that invited my date and me to the party. Some of them whom I hadn't met yet asked me what my name was. I responded with the expectation of a follow-up question like, "Oh, how do you pronounce it again?" (Although I've abandoned the idea that people who are English speakers will know how to because my first name is typical French pronunciation. Instead, I've mourned and have since accepted the horrid variant "Yzu.")

I love my name and its story so much. My mother was reading a book when she was pregnant with me, as she often did; and she transmitted her love for books to me when I was a little girl. She was reading the love story of *Tristan and Iseult*. She ended the book and decided that I would be named like the princess of the story, but she changed the *I* to a *Y*, which I prefer. You can see why it's really meaningful for me. This story is a classic in literature and most people in Belgium and France actually recognize my name and love seeing someone carrying it in modern times. This classic inspired *Romeo and Juliet*. The name Yseult is actually Celtic, which was the original language of the region that is now Ireland.

So, back to my lovely evening: As I answered where my name was from, a white girl listening nearby I guess was so perturbed that she cut me off and said, "No, it's not a Celtic name or an Irish name." I laughed slightly at how confused she was that a Black girl from Africa could carry an Irish name. I was probably ruffling her perception of self and her half-assed knowledge of Ireland.

I didn't bother to answer. One of the guys next to me promptly addressed Beverly (I never got to know her name, just giving her one for context) and said, "Dude, if she says that her name is Celtic, it's probably true." I just got half a giggle out of the whole situation and never bothered to correct Beverly for cutting me off to tell me where my own name was from. Definitely don't be like Beverly. Learn the world we live in and know that things are interconnected. On an interpersonal level, white people owe it to themselves and all other BIPOC around to be aware, informed, and use the tools that we have today so that you don't become like Beverly. It's also the easiest way to make a change. As much as the interpersonal requires a real and genuine investment, it's also easiest in the sense that you get to work on a small and relatable scale of things.

Prioritizing white culture is also contradictory in a way, because most everything that is trendy for white people comes from BIPOC communities: from the Jewish bagel you eat in the morning, to the Native sage and palo santo in your makeshift moon rituals, to the Indian yoga you practice, to even the vegan and vegetarian diets that come from Brown and Black communities. A lot of what people practice or eat daily today are from BIPOC communities, and have been successfully whitewashed to a point of not realizing where it's from.

I'm sure I'm not the only one who cares to know where things come from, and because of that, it drives me insane to see how origin stories are erased. I enjoy learning and understanding more about the world that non-white people are experiencing. It gets tiring answering all the weird questions and reactions I receive from white people, even about something as simple as my name.

On a professional level, exclusion hurts BIPOC in their livelihoods. I'm always angered to see that the question of diversifying a space comes with an assumption that it means that companies will have smaller profits or must lower qualifications to make their space diverse and inclusive. It's a lie that feeds into the white supremacist idea that BIPOC aren't as competent and smart. We aren't in rooms not because we aren't capable, but rather because whiteness is afraid to see visible minorities gain the same resources and status. I'm sure there's a secret fear of real competition, because it's been proven that for a BIPOC person to be in a room with power, we'd have had to work at much higher standards than the white men and women present. There are so many competent BIPOC who don't get the job because they are held to a white status quo that doesn't give space for them to fully engage and thrive as they could.

I think we need to change the perception of diversity in work spaces. Diversity is not charity, and no one is asking for a handout. People are asking to be hired and to lead as they should. Having people in-house that see things differently is a win for a company—you can avoid the major errors that companies make because they don't give space for a culture that equalizes the grounds for BIPOC and allies to speak up. Companies would save so much in PR cleanups and half-assed apology statements if more BIPOC were hired and empowered to speak up. They'd also market to a larger consumer base, whatever the product or service of a company, and they would make more profit. There's power in having awareness about race because your target market now exists across many communities, and not just one.

Take, for instance, popular cosmetic brands in the Belgian market, companies that are a microcosm of what I grew up with. Without having to name anyone specifically, successful cosmetic companies typically catered only to white women.

They've made money by focusing on white and fairer clientele, from their hair products to makeup. For a long time—and I'd even argue now—many of them haven't (or they've slowly started) been at the forefront of casting diverse models for their campaigns (at least not in Belgium), and generally, aside from now-popular specific brands, I still struggle to find a foundation for skin tones like mine. They've narrowed themselves into such a specific clientele and they've succeeded in that space, but what if they had reached Brown and Black clientele early on, and not just when other brands started to pick up on the market of Black, Brown, and non-white women? They likely would have been so much more profitable, especially because Black and Brown communities spend so much on hair and makeup. Taking care of our hair as Black women is "shul" to ourselves; it's a ritual that many Black women practice as self-love, and we spend a lot of money on it.

Applying this perspective in any industry immediately removes that whiff of "charity" for what it means to be inclusive to minority groups. I don't want a hug or handout from a white person or a once-a-year statement that shows "support." I want respect and inclusion so I can easily find the products that I need and want. So that I don't panic when I travel and notice I forgot my shea butter when I'm headed to a predominately white space and realize I'm going to have ashy skin for a few days because there's no "Black/ Ethnic" stores or aisles. Similarly, I don't want the spices and flavors that I use for my dishes to be limited to a designated area that's found on the last shelves of a megastore.

BIPOC at this point are everywhere, and if we aren't, it's not because we don't want to be but because certain environments are set in ways that make it clear that "strangers" aren't welcome. We should make a cultural shift in companies and other spaces with the understanding that as much as it sounds corny to say, diversity *is* wealth. This is also true in friendships, because the people in our lives are windows to a world that we can only have access to by genuinely caring for others.

FOUR

The White Lens

A Bleached Perspective

Recently, a white friend who is a magazine editor, described an instance at work with her white boss. It was a post–Summer 2020 world, and most white-led organizations were feeling pressure to increase outward-facing representation. Our friend described having to convince her boss—who was apparently unable to read the room—to include the work of writers of color for their biggest issue of the year. Eventually, the boss acquiesced, and a Black writer was tapped to write a feature. But upon reading the piece, the white editor seemed to have more critiques than usual, including demanding that the story, about Black fashion designers, contain "more sadness."

This is an example of the many ways that our white lenses blind us and harm others. What *is* the white lens? It's the filter that distorts our beliefs, words, and actions through the idea that whiteness is rightness, and it centers whiteness as the ultimate authority. It's always present if we're white, but our awareness of it varies based on our upbringing and education. Though we've been socialized to normalize it, that doesn't mean it isn't toxic and that we don't need to take responsibility for its impact.

Because the editor had to be convinced to include Black voices in the issue, she was operating under the assumption that her magazine's readership was mostly white, and that white readers didn't really want to read about Blackness or from a Black perspective. Her white lens also assumed that those white readers would only value the perspective of a Black woman if it pulled at emotional strings and contained trauma porn, or the voyeuristic consumption of others' hardships. Given that she wanted the piece oriented toward pain, her white lens erased the story of its nuance and complexity into what she thought Blackness should sound like. This likely had a negative impact not just on the piece but on the writer, too. The editor's decisions were most likely not conscious choices—she was simply acting based on her own perceptions of Blackness and through the filter of her white lens.

This scenario shows up a lot, especially when we want to be applauded for our "good deed" of making the choice to include representation outside of whiteness. But our inclusive efforts, when we can't see past our white lens, can end up causing harm instead.

My own white lens has caused harm to Yseult. In the summer of 2021 we made a Reel, one of Instagram's proprietary video-creating tools, showing the exact scenario that we described in the last chapter: a white woman, played by me, approaching a Black woman, played by Yseult, in a majority-white space. I compliment her on her outfit, to which she responds, "Thank you," and the video goes back and forth with our own internal monologues. My inner self, as the white woman, thinks, "Why is she not saying anything else? I'm a nice white woman, totally cool with her in this space. I don't even see color!" Yseult's inner dialogue reads: "This feels weird. Is she tokenizing me? Why can't I just work?"

We aimed to illustrate the daily, seemingly mundane inter-actions that happen between women of color and white women. We wanted to show that despite my good white intentions, those moments can have a negative impact on women of color. To preempt the comments we knew would come, we wrote, "We know some people might say: 'We can't give compliments anymore?!' But we're trying to illustrate the daily awkwardness between WOC and WW[18]."

Despite our small following at the time, the Reel went viral, and got hundreds of thousands of views. Many white women jumped in to defend giving out compliments, doubling down on their good intentions, and calling for more kindness from Black women, who, they reasoned, should receive their compliments without assuming the worst. For several days, Yseult responded to these women to say that we weren't taking a stand against compliments, but illustrating how they were being received, and that they can feel tokenizing. She likened it to men catcalling women and expecting us to respond gratefully. Despite what the intentions were, this was her perceived reality. And that should really have been the end of that.

Even when Yseult shared her own experience, which deserved to be validated, the white women (and several men) jumped in to center themselves and their intentions over the impact.

How did *my* white lens show up in this experience? While I was excited about the engagement and the subsequent growth to our Instagram following from the Reel going viral, Yseult was not. I hadn't considered just how exhausting the hundreds of repetitive comments, invalidating her truth, would feel for her. In my excitement about superficial metrics, I was not cen-

---

18   WW = white women.

tering what is most important, which is that our work doesn't harm anyone, especially Yseult.

A White-Flavored and White-Favored World

Up until a few years ago, I never considered that my viewpoint was distinctly white. Like most white people, I believed that I consumed the media, education, and news around me objectively, as any other person would. I never considered that my perception of the world was racialized. Over the years, and only with dedicated unlearning and relearning, the white-centeredness of our society and my lens has become glaringly obvious to me. We live in a white-flavored and a white-*favored* world. Though non-white people exist within that society, it's usually in a way that's secondary.

Our news anchors, our movie stars, and our textbooks and teachers create the universe that most white people come to accept as the default. Many of us will point to prominent and wealthy Black people like Barack Obama, Oprah, and Beyoncé to try to disprove our society's racial hierarchy, as if their singular success could make up for centuries of stolen land and labor, medical bias, the wealth gap, police brutality, and so on. I think we use these examples of Black prominence because we so badly want to believe in the myth of meritocracy—that if we all work hard enough, we'll earn what we deserve. We want to believe that as white people we have zero responsibility in bridging the gaps that we have created between us and people of color.

Our ignorance doesn't have a neutral impact on those around us, as the magazine editor example shows. It's our responsibility as aspiring allies to recognize how whiteness has blinded us and that our lens is not an unbiased one. Thinking back through the years, I can recall so many instances of how this showed up in my own behavior, and of course, it still does.

Even while I'm trying to shatter the white lens from my consciousness, it reveals itself in my language in ways that Yseult will always catch. A few years ago, we were on a call with a white-owned fashion brand that wanted to partner with us, which we were open to since they'd been very vocal about their anti-racism work.

On the call, acknowledging their efforts, I said, "I've noticed that you've done a lot of work to help people of color." Afterward, Yscult and I were debriefing about the meeting when she said, "Hannah, did you notice that you said 'helping'? Why is it 'helping' when they're working with people of color, but 'collaborating' or 'partnering with' when it's with other white people?"

She was right. My white lens showed itself in that moment: the white-savior idea that we're here to "save" people of color, as if we can swoop in and grant BIPOC the privilege of working with us. I'm grateful that we have built enough trust between us where Yseult takes the time to point out to me these nuances in my language and perspective, because even though it's subtle, it reveals the still-ingrained superiority of whiteness.

When I worked at a popular women's magazine, there was a massive mood board in our conference room papered solely with images of white women—white faces, white hair, white bodies. According to that mood board, the magazine was a brand by and for white women alone. When a short-lived sister brand was created—an English-language publication for Latina readers that existed in print from 2012-2015—it was not from the desire to serve a Latina audience, but rather created as a vehicle to capture more dollars from advertisers to market their ads specifically to the Latina community, who hold tremendous spending power but are often overlooked. Needless to say, this venture wasn't a success. The Latina brand went purely digital in 2015 and stopped publishing any new content.

While the mood board at that women's magazine might look

different today, including more images of WOC, as they've been intentional about doing as of this writing, every editor in chief of said magazine has been white, as has every CEO since the company was founded. While none of this is surprising, it suggests that most white people think there is nothing wrong with continuous white leadership and assumes that white people have the gift of a universal perspective, able to speak to and from many points of view—as if whiteness is a blank slate, rather than a very specific POV.

Decentering Whiteness

Coming to terms with our own white lens can come as a shock: a reality shift where you recognize you've been living in a parallel universe. Some have likened it to the moment Neo takes the red pill in *The Matrix* and begins to see the systems of control that have existed the whole time. That whiteness is prioritized in our society is not accidental—it's by design. There are so many racial disparities that I grew up accepting because I believed that they were just the "way things were," like the way we were sorted in middle school.

We've been brainwashed to believe that racism is just about prejudice, when it's about power. Racism is not a question of whether you like someone or not or smile at them in the grocery store. Our society was and continues to be structured by and for white people and for our benefit—all on the backs of Indigenous, Black, and Brown people, for centuries. That is not a truth we're willing to face, and the white lens makes it easy for us to ignore.

Niceness will not shift these institutions or the lasting impact that they've had on non-white people. White people have long had the power to decide what our society looks like and how resources are allocated. We've bought into the illusion of a level playing field, when in reality, America subscribes deeply to a racial caste system. Isabel Wilkerson, author of *Caste: The Origins of Our Discontents*, says, "Caste is the bones, race is the skin,"[19] to describe the solid yet out-of-sight structure by which we group and assign worth based on skin tone.

Sometimes it just takes one aha moment for the lens to start to shift into focus. One of the most impactful books that I've read is Michelle Alexander's book *The New Jim Crow: Mass Incarceration in the Age of Colorblindness*. The book draws parallels between slavery, the Jim Crow era, and our current system of mass incarceration, which confines more Black and Brown men in prison than were ever enslaved. It's a shocking, sobering look at the prison pipeline, and the tactics used by politicians to target, criminalize, and imprison Black and Brown men intentionally for political gain. By branding so many Black and Brown men as felons, our government prevents the formerly incarcerated from getting decent jobs, housing, or basic humanity for their *lifetime*, while also stripping them of their right to vote.

Ms. Alexander writes that America's prison population was low and comparable to other developed countries in the late '70s and early '80s, and that drug use, which was always pretty equal among races, was actually dropping when the Reagan administration announced the War on Drugs. She writes that the CIA was helping to fund some of the Nicaraguan drug cartels that were funneling illicit drugs into the United States. In order to distract lower-class, struggling whites from blaming rich whites for their problems, Reagan needed to divert their attention away from him and his elite peers and find a new scapegoat: Black people. Knowing people of color tended to vote Democrat, the War on Drugs was targeted specifically to Black and Brown communities, even though white people were using the same drugs at the same rates. Police were given monetary incentives

---

19   https://bookshop.org/books/caste-oprah-s-book-club-the-origins-of-our-discontents-9780593230251/9780593230251.

to target Black and Brown men, and locked them up at astonishing rates. The media propagated ideas and images of "welfare queens," "crack babies," and "Black-on-Black crime," creating harmful stereotypes of Black communities that still exist today.

The goal was clear: disenfranchise the Black vote for white power. In turn, destroy Black communities, and blame them for the very circumstances that white people created. The American government was complicit every step of the way.

This example of how white supremacy operates and influences should inspire a perspective shift from the one we've been fed: that the government is color-blind, that criminals look a certain way, that Black folks take "advantage of the system," and that we should trust in law and order. *The New Jim Crow* helped bust up my worldview, which had previously been something like this: "Yes, some people are racist, but our country is fair, and luckily, I'm living during a time where everyone has equal opportunity to prosper. As long as we're all kind to each other, everything will work out!" I was clueless.

I was sickened reading *The New Jim Crow*, learning that our society could allow this to happen to our own citizens. If white people had been the targets of the War on Drugs, drug use wouldn't *be* a crime. It would be a public health crisis (see: the opioid epidemic).

When I shared my outrage with Yseult, her reaction was: "Of course."

"*Oh my God*, Yseult. The War on Drugs…Nicaragua…the CIA," I bumbled.

"Yeah," Yseult said measuredly. "You didn't know about this?"

I didn't. That's another example of my white lens: sharing what I've read about racism with those who have experienced it, directly or indirectly, as if it's new to them. My degree of shock is directly tied to my degree of naivete. I am immensely privileged to learn about this part of our history in a book and not to have had to directly experience it. What's important in this context, then, is what I *do* with the new information.

Our history books tend to gloss over or omit completely the horrors that our country has committed against others. For example, I didn't learn about the concentration camps that imprisoned 120,000 Japanese people in America, most of them American citizens, in the 1940s until a Japanese American friend told me about the camps in my early twenties. Even though I heard him, my brain didn't want to believe him. The lie that I'd been sold about America—that we are a just, moral country, so unlike every other—was so strong that it was like he was talking about another planet. If this was true, why hadn't I known about it?

After reading *The Color of Law: A Forgotten History of How Our Government Segregated America* by Richard Rothstein, a book about the impact of government-enforced neighborhood segregation, racism in real estate, and redlining, I was stunned by the long history of covert and overt tactics to keep Black people away from white neighborhoods. The author sheds light on the restrictive covenants that prevented the sale of homes to Black buyers, as well as the intimidation and ruthless violence Black homeowners faced. White people in power would limit the neighborhoods that Black people could live in, driving up demand, so that they could charge Black renters twice that of white renters. Additionally, there have been studies done showing that appraisers undervalue homes that they know are Black-owned.[20] Like every other institution in America, the real estate and housing markets have a long history of racism, disenfranchisement, and even government-sanctioned violence.

---

20   https://www.cbsnews.com/news/freddie-mac-home-appraisal-housing-discrimination-black-homeowner/#:~:text=Researchers%20found%20that%2012.5%25%20of,Latino%20areas%2C%20the%20analysis%20found.

Which, of course, is not how I, as a white woman, had previously seen it. In my mind, moving from place to place had been only a question of where we wanted to live and if we could afford it. Before being with my husband, I never had to consider: "Will there be people who look like me in this neighborhood? Will I face discrimination in the application process? Will neighbors look at me suspiciously, or call the cops on me? Can I jog in peace?" These are all questions my husband has to ask and carefully consider (and that I, as his partner, do, too).

Being able to acknowledge the white lens is key to being an ally, because it will always be there. When I can recognize that my perceptions and prejudices exist because I'm looking through a distortion, then the reality of things can become clearer. I'm also then better equipped to take responsibility for my white lens harming others.

The white lens is so omnipresent that we forget that it—and its gendered cousin misogyny—is not that special at all. The white lens is something white women, especially, can relate to, because they know what it's like to be living in a parallel reality with men who experience preferential treatment in nearly all areas of society.

We have a culture that centers white men in all ways. Voting rights, reproductive rights, and work culture—anywhere there was and still is inequality and inequity regarding women's humanity in this world, BIPOC have experienced the same dynamic, but it's racialized.

As women, we have all experienced trying to explain what catcalling feels like only to be met with mansplaining and the "It was just a compliment—you don't have to see the harm in everything" response. This energy focuses on men's feelings and their perception of women around them. They're seeing that moment through a male gaze, one where they don't understand what it feels like to fear that a man could get upset and violent because you didn't answer the way he wanted. That's the male gaze.

The white lens is exactly the same energy and process. Because you haven't been in these social situations, you can't really understand and see beyond your own limited experience. Kind of like when there's a seemingly kind white person who "doesn't see race," but they'll innately understand that there's a power dynamic at play. They can weaponize their whiteness when they feel upset about something. It happens all the time and it's fascinating to watch when white tears are triggered, just like a mechanical clock.

I feel so much rage when I see BIPOC put in danger for dumb reasons because of the white lens. For instance, when a disagreement could be resolved with a conversation, but a white person will choose to call the police, ignoring the dynamic. Cops and Black people are a bad mix, we've established that, but we're still encountering "really nice white people" calling the police on Black people because they think it is right. BUT FOR WHOM? That's the white lens! Just like a guy has the luxury of running in the middle of the park at night with his headphones without even thinking about what may happen. I have girlfriends who jog but have to take so many precautions to stay safe: only have one earphone on, have some mace just in case, or avoid running at night because the odds aren't in our favor.

The gaslighting that results from the white lens is what makes this conversation relevant, because I should be believed and my experience validated when I share my story. Instead, what happens most of the time is that I'm characterized as being dramatic and not wanting peace because I'm not "playing nice." The more white people are open to other people's experiences and viewpoints, the easier it will be for them to identify the white lens and limit the amount of harm it causes for the BIPOC in their community.

The Burden the White Lens Puts on BIPOC

From my personal experience as a Black person, I have been forced to understand the white lens, and I'm left to deal with its consequences. To a certain extent I'm fine with that, because *life*. The joke is when white people who know nothing and are blinded by their own issues ask you how they can help—it's like a cat offering to teach a fish how to swim. Sir, no, I'm good. The focus has to be changed, and white people need to understand that as much as they are part of the problem, the solution is for them to figure out how much internalized racism they need to unpack and deal with before trying to pose as experts.

I'm of a mature age and have experience that helps me speak on this, but I do not proclaim to be an expert in knowing how to fix and explain all aspects and dynamics of racism. I also want everyone who reads my words to understand that I speak for myself and not everyone will agree. But I believe that there's power in sharing stories and making others feel seen and empowered, not by having fully digested solutions, but offering how I process and deal so that they may feel like their experiences aren't isolated.

I want white people to start moving in that spirit, too—not posing as experts and saviors, because they can't help me fix something they can barely see, but rather addressing and unpacking whatever it is that's influencing their vision of the world. They can ask: Is this perpetuating white supremacy? Am I feeding into it? What are my shortcomings? I believe that that's the best step forward, because white people can then support each other, grow together, and help their own community, and thus create safer spaces for BIPOC to be in. You'd have people who are more aware, less afraid to speak up, and more willing to stand up for beliefs that equalize BIPOC.

But so often, the burden is put on BIPOC to deal with the

difference in lenses. We have to do intellectual and emotional gymnastics not to lose our shit. And this doesn't just include the small things, but big, essential things, too, like medical racial bias. It's a tough pill to swallow when you realize that certain medical devices are made to measure white skin as the default, and because of that, Black people don't benefit from good care and can come close to dying from preventable health issues.

There are also more interpersonal situations, like when you're out with friends and express your discomfort when you see that the establishment is racist, but your dear friend brushes you off as if you have no idea what you're seeing. This, to me, is when the white lens is the most harmful. It's a societal issue, yes, but in this moment it's also made personal. When you're with a friend who doesn't seem to have adjusted their lens, it's up to you to engage in an awkward conversation that tests your friendship.

I've tried to imagine how white people feel when they learn about the white lens for the first time. For example, what does a white woman feel when wrapping her mind around the idea that her whiteness isn't just a color, and that a lot of people are suffering from a society that has made whiteness a weapon of oppression? The human in me understands that this realization must be difficult and scary.

It's a parallel reality: the shock, the confusion. I find it even more incredible because even if there's so much put in place to maintain these lies and distorted realities, it's not like it's a secret. There are so many scholars and people who have been working to uncover systems that support racism and racial bias. It's not like when a child is growing up and everyone collectively keeps the secret of Santa Claus. The evidence is there and is widely available.

I sometimes wonder what it would feel like to live in a world that says that you are the default in absolutely everything.

White people, through the white lens, believe that everything is in their image. They are considered the ones that brought civilization to non-white worlds. Sometimes it feels like if someone white wasn't there, did it even happen? White supremacy, through its colonization and slave trade, has halted and disrupted so many civilizations. We will never see what the world could have been without white supremacy claiming and invading every place it touched. I know that when I speak like this, it makes white people feel scared and worried that one day minorities will treat them the way white society has treated us. But no one wants revenge. Rather, I want to see real stories, diverse points of view, and equal access to the pen that is used to write history.

I am so lucky to be able to leave and go to my homeland in Rwanda, where everyone is like me. I don't have to worry there that someone is going to think I'm trying to steal something, or that I will be spoken to with disrespect for no other reason than being a Black woman. It's an incredible weight that I feel lifted when I'm in Rwanda. I'm not the Black girl; I am a young woman, seen for who I am past the color of my skin.

A bit of critical thinking is enough to make sense of these things. As a Black woman, I want no handouts or help, I just want a world that makes it possible for me to be the main character without having to fight or do heavy advocacy, to get to have space to just be a human, and be seen and celebrated as such.

Cleansing Your Lens

We must dismantle the white lens. Racism is a scary word for a lot of white people, because people have extreme images of what it means and they fear being punished and attacked. In reality, most BIPOC do a lot of work to lean in and give space for reconciliation. We need to understand the depth of how white supremacy shows up on a societal and personal level.

You can be working in fashion and consider yourself open-minded and peaceful. You can have people of color around you, travel, go brunching. But as innocent or as worldly or as well-intentioned as you may be, you will still have racist thoughts. I've even had to address and dismantle *my own* self-hate that comes from white supremacy. How do we perpetuate white supremacy through what's normalized for us?

Seeing racism as an either/or choice is the reason why there's so much denial about the individual participation in upholding it, which erases the nuances and subtleties of how racism shows up. We all have the tainted mark of racism or prejudice; it manifests differently depending on if you are white or BIPOC. Whether we are conscious of how these things manifest will predict how we decide to react. I'm thinking of people who are white but not hateful—not tiki torch marchers or white hoods–wearing racists—the common Joes and Janes that just don't realize their own impact but are aware enough to want to talk about it.

The truth is that most white people that I'm going to encounter are going to be in the middle of this racism spectrum. Biases in your mind, head, and heart is normal. And this will reveal itself in your fears and comments.

The question isn't: "Am I racist or not?" It's: "Am I perpetuating racism in the way I live my life?"

The reframing of this question makes it less about yourself, and more about understanding what another person is going through and being able to amplify their voice in the struggle. Decenter yourself and avoid asking, "How am I feeling?" because, ultimately, anti-racism work is about others and their feelings.

Every time you feel uncomfortable standing up for what is right, you have to remember that someone like me is uncomfortable all the time because my Blackness is visible. There's no place where I'm not thinking about the fact that I'm Black, not because I'm obsessively thinking about it, but rather because the world that I live in makes a point to remind me through blunt and subtle racism. It's part of my reality. Being conscious of my reality results in an awareness that can help me feel more secure. Putting that into perspective when you are battling with your discomfort may help decenter yourself and your white lens when it comes to these issues.

The lens also has to be inclusive of communities and "isms" that aren't as obvious or are often left out of people's advocacy. As part of my identity, I am also Rwandan, queer, and Jewish. I wear a Star of David around my neck and talk inclusively about antisemitism while speaking about racism. It has felt like in much of advocacy we leave out antisemitism because Jewish people are thought to be a white group of people. Otherness and oppression aren't only exclusive to visible minorities. Jewish people are white, Asian, Black, and so on. When you have a group of people that cannot congregate to pray in peace without needing police, there's something there to include and talk about.

My synagogue, Central Synagogue, always has police officers out front on Shabbat Shul, which is a clear sign that there's a real threat to the Jewish community. More visibly Jewish communities, like Hasidic or Orthodox, experience more direct threats, and they are easier targets for harassment, attacks, and killings. Hannah and I hosted a class where I proposed that as someone trying to become an ally, you should also include fighting antisemitism. There are so many antisemitic attacks on the Jewish community here in New York. A *New York Times* article reported that Hasidic communities experienced more than half of the antisemitic hate crimes reported in the year of 2021—the highest in decades.[21]

Cleansing the lens is being willing to challenge all that we think is normal, and pushing further to make sure that we are

---

21 https://www.nytimes.com/2022/04/26/nyregion/antisemitic-attacks-new-york.html.

being discerning and inclusive on this journey. I think that there's a popularity contest when it comes to the minority groups that white people want to be seen as close to: Black people are the ultimate gold star. We are visible so people don't have to question that you're "a nice white person." Personally, it doesn't mean much to me when folks are "pro-Black" if they are not willing to stand up when the Asian community, Arab community, or Jewish community is victim to hate that originates from white supremacist ideology. I don't think I can feel safe and happy if I see another group suffering because they are othered, whether I identify with that group or not.

We'll end this chapter with steps to recognize and decenter the white lens.

Questions and Suggestions to Recognize and Decenter the White Lens

- **Where is your white lens the most prominent?**

- **Does the white lens show up in the books or magazines that you read, the people you follow, or the news that you consume?**

- **How does the white lens show up in your place of work? How does your white lens impact those around you, and potentially cause harm?**

- **We invite you to question societal narratives and definitions of success. Who defines success? Who do those prescriptions exclude?**

- **What's your relationship to whiteness? What kinds of images of whiteness did you see growing up? Were your teachers white? Your bosses? What was lost from the omnipresence of whiteness?**

- Let's play a game called *What Do You See?* Picture:
  - A family on a road trip
  - An ambitious, kind woman
  - A family adopting a dog
  - A single, hardworking guy who enjoys carpentry
  - A beautiful couple strolling on the beach
  - A culinary travel destination
  - A violinist
  - A horse rider
  - Your group of friends

- If the reflexive images that appeared for you were primarily white or European, think about why.

FIVE

What Is an Ally and
Who Gets To Be One?

The term *allyship* has become so popular, it's used like an Instagram filter that's supposed to highlight your best features. But the reality is that there's a lack of honest talk about what allyship means or looks like. Being an ally isn't knowing that racism exists or that it's bad—it's actually working to apply those beliefs to everything you're involved with and care about.

I look at how white people participate in things like recycling and animal rights, and how much more intentional they are about those things than being anti-racist. They don't go around saying they care about the planet and then not recycle. White vegans can be the most passionate people ever, but ask them about social justice and their faces turn pale and the silence becomes heavy. It's uncomfortable, but my point is that people should bring the same energy and care toward allyship.

Allyship means engaging in conversations with BIPOC friends about things that are happening in the news or how they feel about these issues. It's normal to check on your friends in all ways possible, and this extends to ways they might be dealing with racism if you have a close relationship. Due diligence is required when it comes to racial issues. We all desire connection as human beings, and reaching out and offering support reminds us that friendship can be the space for hope and reconciliation.

I have fine-tuned my radar from years of seeing and experiencing all kinds of people on the racism spectrum to the point that I can see when someone isn't being genuine from a mile away. Real allyship is about doing something to address the injustice that exists around you and speaking up and advocating, even when it feels or looks scary. I've often said discomfort doesn't kill, and white people or any ally should expect to feel uncomfortable. Growth only happens when we are able to be uncomfortable and let in change by addressing *why* it's so uncomfortable.

Embracing those truths—that allyship isn't easy or comfortable, and that growth often feels painful or scary in the moment—are so key for me as an aspiring ally.

We treat allyship as if it's a permanent identity or hashtag that we can claim, but it's much more complex because it requires different considerations and actions for each individual and community. It's not up to me if I'm an ally. In my friendship with Yseult, it's up to Yseult. We were speaking with a journalist when I first heard Yseult clarify this. She said, "White people can't claim to be allies before we deem that they're being present for us." It showed me why it's paradoxical for white people to identify as allies, since it's often something that we claim from people of color that they haven't given us. Some days, I'm a better ally than others. I don't believe that I or anyone else gets to self-assign the designation; instead, it's the individual or community to whom one wishes to be an ally that gets to decide if it's allyship or not.

If even talking about race with our friends feels too scary, we

will never be able to be allies, let alone articulate or act upon witnessing injustice. Allyship is a muscle that we need to learn to use daily.

Proximity Is Not Allyship

This bears repeating: *proximity is not allyship.* If our best friend/partner/colleague is gay/Black/Indigenous/a person with a disability[22] or marginalized in any way, we are not necessarily an ally to that community just because we're close to someone who belongs to it. Hopefully we're at a place where we know that the words "But some of my best friends are Black!" is laughable because it means very little.

Being friends and business partners with Yseult and being in an interracial marriage does not automatically make me an ally, nor does having other people of color in my life. Their presence does not prove to myself or others that I am a good, open-minded person.

If we use our proximity to others as proof of our allyship while we do *nothing* else, we are tokenizing them and mistaking what allyship means. Being around people who identify differently than us can be an opportunity for more empathy, wider perspectives, and hopefully, impactful action, but only if the trust exists to have fruitful and transparent conversations. However, it often seems like white people who have friends/family members/colleagues of color use them as proof that we're allies, instead of questioning if we're actually being one. If those people of color don't feel like they can genuinely express themselves and their experiences to us, how real is the relationship? As we've said, there is no neutral impact that white people have on people of color. We're either helpful or harmful, and our pres-

---

22 Some people prefer "person with a disability" while others prefer "disabled person," but it is important to ask each individual how they'd like to be identified.

ence as white people alone typically *isn't* helpful, based on our history and the power dynamics of white supremacy.

Before you roll your eyes or get angry at me, please know that I don't believe as white people we're all inherently bad. I'm pointing out that there is often a gap between what we think our impact is as allies and what our actual impact is, and I want to bring awareness to that. (And no, I also don't believe that white people should self-flagellate about our awfulness because that's also unhelpful and self-centering.)

I remember trying to have a conversation with a white woman at work about race after she said something that was anti-Black. I approached the conversation with her as delicately and kindly as I could, and asked her why she'd made the comment. She got flustered, and rambled to me that her daughter's college roommate was gay, which she thought was "great" and would be "such a good experience" for her daughter. This bumbling, baffling exchange, where she seemed to grasp at straws for any proximity to anyone from any marginalized community showed me a few things:

1. She assumed that her "acceptance" for one member of a marginalized group proved her acceptance for all.

2. This tenuous, secondhand proximity to one gay woman meant to her that she was an ally.

3. Her daughter's gay roommate existed as a learning lesson for her straight daughter.

4. This woman believed that there was nothing left to learn about racism, allyship, or activism simply because she thought it was "great" that her daughter had a gay roommate.

5. When a white person believes that they've been accused of discrimination, defensiveness is the first impulse.

I wish it was uncommon for conversations about race with white peers to enter this Twilight Zone territory, but her reaction is pretty typical—I've likely had the same one. Admittedly, I know little about this woman's personal life or history—I cannot judge the whole of who she is, and it's not up to me to. And while I desire to be far away on the spectrum from her when it comes to racism, we're still alike. Pointing fingers at others doesn't make me an ally either.

I share this exchange to illustrate the ridiculousness of how badly we all want to seem like good white people by emphasizing the relationships we have with marginalized groups, no matter how weak they are, and how reactive we become when our "allyship" is called into question.

If I stood beside a beautiful unicorn, would I be considered a unicorn?

Probably not, unless there are a bunch of other people doing it around me and reinforcing my behavior as normal. That's how I feel when white people try to show their proximity to BIPOC. I mean, I'm being funny and light about it, but I do think the phenomenon is bizarre.

When white people rely on proximity, I think it shows that we've ignored the real conversation about what allyship means and looks like. As a Black woman, it's easy for me to grasp what allyship is, but isn't obvious if you're white. As a Black person, I have such high standards expected of me in all areas of my life, that I know I would have to prove myself before I was considered an ally. It's conditioned in me that I have to work twice as hard to be taken seriously. I understand that I need to be genuine and shouldn't claim allyship without real work and action to show for it. But clearly that isn't obvious to everyone, because we still have to explain and address that proximity isn't allyship. I'm giggling as I'm writing this because sometimes it feels a little unbelievable. I find it silly and alarming that something that feels so obvious must be explained.

Another relatable example of how people try to use proximity is when men say they support women and are feminists because they have mothers, sisters, or wives. I personally have never heard a guy say, "Yeah, I know what you mean. I'm a women's rights ally, I have a mom," but I know that line of thinking exists. I mean, that's so much of a stretch, my arm is broken just thinking about it.

Okay, I'll stop with the jokes. It's my awkward attempt to deal with this. I find it insulting and diminishing when white people use proximity to BIPOC to justify their allyship and understanding of people's struggles. I don't want to be an excuse for someone to try and avoid their own accountability. It also ignores the fact that not all BIPOC have conversations about race with their white friends. If simply being friends is equivocated with being allies, the reasons for being friends may have an ulterior motive, and that's an icky feeling to have in a space that's supposed to feel good and safe. I've recently started wondering if I've had white people claim me as a friend for appearances, but how would I know? I'd like to think that wouldn't happen with any of my close friends. When white people use proximity, it's a clear manifestation of how little you understand and see the person in front of you, and it reinforces the false sense of BIPOC being a monolith because it suggests that that one Black, Brown, or Jewish friend represents all of our experiences.

I've seen white proximity manifest in a couple different ways. Like Hannah shared in her example, white people will sometimes try to dig up their third cousin's five-times-removed's best friend in elementary school or the like when someone confronts them with problematic behavior. I can always feel the heaviness of discomfort in the air when this happens. I let the person wear themselves out with all of their mental gymnastics. And then I breathe and reply as calmly as possible: "But still, what you said was racist."

White proximity can also exist on a cultural level, when a white person feels they understand something from our culture from the briefest or most tangential of encounters. I think of it like that first draft of the first essay you had to write in college. It was unresearched trash! A white person will sum up what they think they know and may have seen from a thirty-second YouTube video to make a connection to a person of color. It's funny and cringey.

I'll never forget when my brother and I met this white girl in a bar—she'd overheard us speaking in French. We are both Black, obviously, and she was from somewhere in the Eastern EU. As my brother and I caught up and bantered in French, she came over to us and cheerfully asked, "OMG, are you guys speaking French? I speak it, too!" She then smoothly switched to French with a slight accent, and we gleefully responded. We thought she might be from either France or Belgium.

She called over her American boyfriend and told him, "Hey, babe, they speak French." Up until then, Ricky and I were not weirded out. Then, as is typical with these encounters, I was kind of zoned out and wasn't paying close attention while Ricky was still engaging with the girl. Suddenly, I saw that he had a strange facial reaction to whatever she'd said. I knew in that moment that it would be something ridiculous. I mean, I know my brother.

She warmly wished us goodbye, gave a hug to Ricky, and I politely stayed seated to show that I don't hug. Then with an excited grin, I asked why he reacted like he did: "What did she say?"

Ricky said, "Dude, she said she spoke French, but not Creole."

Now I understood the face and utter confusion from Ricky

113

a few moments before. I asked him, "But why? Did she know we'd lived in Belgium?" He said yes.

So somewhere, at some point of time in this young lady's life, she learned that French was spoken in France and Belgium, but then probably read a summarized history lesson on France and its old colonies, one being Haiti, where they speak French Creole. She put two and two together and decided that because we were Black, we must have been Haitian and probably spoke Creole.

Ricky and I died laughing…that was the funniest thing. Random as hell. Just to continue my metaphor, it was like reading a sloppy first-draft essay you hand in knowing you half-assed it—I've had so many situations like this where a white person knows two unconnected facts and hands you something that feels just so half-thought, but they do it so confidently that you catch yourself self-doubting for a second.

Another example is my encounters with white people who have visited the continent of Africa. The second I say I am from Rwanda I know I'll be forced into a conversation that's not casual or relaxed. Often, I'm asked about the traumatic events of the 1994 genocide against the Tutsis. After twenty-eight years, it seems that they haven't read a single article to know what's happened since. That's at best; at worst I'm asked, "Who did you lose?" or "What side are you on?" It shocks me because it's not something white people would feel good or comfortable opening up about to someone they don't know at all. Imagine I meet a white American and the minute they tell me that they are from the US I say, "Oh, wow, so how are things since segregation? How do you feel about the senseless killing of Black Americans in your country?" The idea is that African countries stay frozen in time and are stuck in events where the narrative focuses on our downfalls and hardship. Americans couldn't imagine being asked such a thing because they see themselves as coming from a great nation. The luxury of being white is not having these horrible things define and stick with you everywhere you go.

I thought about this when I first met Olya, a dear friend of mine. She shared with me that she was from Serbia. At the time, I had never met anyone from Serbia and decided that if I wanted to connect with her on a deeper level, I had to look up more about the people and place she was from. I googled a bit and engaged in things that I had found, and it brought me more insight into who she was. She came from a country I knew nothing about and wasn't taught about in school, so this motivated me to find out more about her.

Another type of encounter that happens is because I'm African, white people expect that I should know someone from anywhere in Africa. Or they suddenly are the experts of the whole continent that comprises fifty-four countries and thousands of languages—sometimes hundreds in just one country—because they once visited one place. Just because "Rebecca" visited Mali for a culture exchange from her church program meant to "save African children from hunger," I am expected to listen to her expertise on the whole continent and her theories about why that particular country is "the best," compared to my own country, which they have never set foot in. It's insulting and dehumanizing at worst, and at best, it's comedic gold.

I think that this idea of having proximity to something that you don't know and can't admit to comes from the toxic teaching and idea that whiteness knows all and is expert on everything. Tea was stolen from India, but now England has the caucasity[23] to call themselves a tea country. They don't grow tea there! I have seen fields of tea, and it's the most beautiful thing ever, but it most definitely does not exist in England—pardon the truth.

My white friends, there's a real freedom in letting go of

23   Caucasity: the audacity of Caucasians.

the idea that as a white person you're an expert. Instead, why not spend more time having necessary conversations and nourishing growth toward true allyship? This vulnerability also gives space for people to naturally assist or guide you in your growth. It's not that hard to let go of, but it's obviously complicated, because as humans it's in our nature to want to be seen as good and right. I just roll my eyes at these encounters and wonder how weird and uncomfortable people must feel in these moments when they think and want to act like they are a unicorn just because they're seated next to one. They are hoping and praying nobody notices, I guess.

Performative Allyship Versus Active Allyship

I like to say I'm an *aspiring* ally. If I imagine myself as working toward allyship rather than believe that I've already arrived, I'm much more motivated. Being an aspiring ally implies sustained action. The idea of never "arriving" to allyship might be frustrating for you, but think about it like you would any relationship—it requires continuous work.

Performative allyship, on the other hand, is like fool's gold. It might look good on the surface, but it has no value. It's when action is taken that appears to look like allyship, but it has no impact or purpose other than elevating the person performing it. We saw so many examples of this in the summer of 2020, after George Floyd's murder led to our country's most recent racial reckoning. It seemed every brand, influencer, and layperson posted their pledges on social media to "listen and learn" about racism. Some companies pledged millions of dollars to the Black community and promised to engage in anti-racism work. A few years later, while there does *appear* to be nominal progress in the global dialogue about race, a lot of the promises made have been empty ones. Black lives continue to be less important to companies and white people than white lives.

White-owned lifestyle, clothing, and beauty brands showing models of color in their ads, on their sites, and on their social media, but not addressing their own toxic company culture that causes real harm to people of color is another example of performative allyship. Prior to June 2020, we'd reached out to many of these kinds of brands, offering our services to help their companies be more inclusive. For the most part, to borrow a line from *Clueless*, we were brutally rebuffed. Very few companies saw the value in doing behind-the-scenes work to make their workplaces more equitable. Empty promises that are not backed up by continuous action and accountability, and are only made during states of emergency, do not move the needle toward justice.

In 2020, white people read *White Fragility*. We watched *13th* on Netflix. And then, it seemed, we called it a day. We saw the numbers in our podcast downloads spike in the summer of 2020 and then drop by about half.

On my own journey, I've learned that being an ally is not just noticing that "things are really messed up" and continuing on with my life. It's also not sharing all the information that I'm learning with people of color and expecting them to be a sounding board for me. Being an ally requires constant effort and courage—courage because white supremacy has convinced us that speaking up *about* white supremacy is dangerous for white people. There is no real risk for us to call out racism, but there *is* risk to people of color when we don't.

We all have influence that we often underestimate, whether it's with our partners, our families, friends, or colleagues. Aspiring allyship can start at the kitchen table. Hopefully, we have the ears of those that love us the most. Some of the conversations that I've had that were the most difficult at first, but then the most impactful, have been with my own family. Being in an interracial marriage, it is imperative to me that my immediate family are aspiring allies. I've shared books with them, invited them into our courses, and I've seen incredible ripple effects from their willingness to learn and do better.

Working toward allyship does not have to be a grand gesture. It can be as simple as having a conversation that scares you. A white friend of mine who manages apartment buildings across the country recently hired a Black woman in another market to work on her team as a marketing associate. From stories that she shared with me, it sounded like this woman didn't feel seen, and there was tension between them that my friend didn't know how to approach. I suggested that she ask her new employee how the company could support her as a Black woman. My friend said she couldn't imagine asking her such a question—it felt too uncomfortable and scary to acknowledge her employee's race.

But months later, when she finally met her colleague in person, my friend asked: "What can we do to support you as a Black woman at this company?" She said her colleague shared with her that no employer had ever asked her that, and they ended up having a productive conversation about her thoughts on the company, and what she might need going forward. My friend said she was *terrified* to bring up race, but it ended up being an incredibly transparent and transformative exchange, and it gave her courage to keep asking what her employees needed and be more empathetic to them. On a business trip to another market, she asked the employees who were new mothers if they had places to pump—and they hesitantly admitted that they didn't. She resolved to create private spaces for them to pump at work so that they didn't have to do it in bathroom stalls. "These conversations have had such a big impact in our company," she told me. It all starts with having the courage to start a dialogue.

Yseult often refers to our different experiences as living parallel lives—our experiences in this world so often do not intersect. There is much to be learned if we just ask and don't assume. So many white people are terrified of these simple questions, but who really benefits if we don't talk about race? We, the white people, do!

When I worked at a big media company, I started an allyship group for employees to create space for conversation about racism in the workplace, to bring awareness to what employees of color were facing at the company, and to build a framework for how white employees could be aspiring allies. The meetings, like the ones in my living room that laid the groundwork for *Kinswomen*, were slow to start. Some white members of the group were ignorant or in denial of the experiences that employees of color were having at the company. I asked my friends of color at work if they would be willing to share their experiences at work (anonymously, so as not to jeopardize their jobs), so that we could then share those experiences at our monthly meetings. They were more than willing, and also agreed to my sharing them in this book. Some of the things they said were:

"Even despite my years of experience (more than my white counterparts), my ideas and contributions were constantly dismissed and received with contempt daily. It felt like I was a junior editor all over again: I had to 'ask' to go to events, my stories were often overedited, and my ideas for WOC-focused stories were presented out of context."

"My team would barely say good morning to me, yet constantly chat with each other about 'exclusive' topics they assumed I had no context about. Then, they'd be surprised when I could hold my own in the conversation."

"Even when I was asked to write pieces specifically for WOC, my editor would literally challenge me on every detail despite having no grasp of the terms, trends, or products these stories were intended to serve. It was honestly like whitewashing so she could understand better."

After these comments and others were presented at our monthly meeting, the white attendees expressed shock and sadness. Our aim was to illustrate what we were subjecting our colleagues to, though of course, this just scratched the surface.

I was scared to ask my work friends about their experiences, too. I did not want them to have to relive moments that were traumatic. But after building trust, I was surprised to see that they were eager to share. They wanted their truth heard.

I realize that when I talk about allyship and racism, some people spend more time on the definition of a word than using their common sense to understand what it means. I find myself having to dissect language that I know we commonly apply to other types of advocacy. Like, having to explore the idea of performative versus active allyship baffles me. I wish the focus could be on making real change rather than spending precious time reminding people that they can't just say they care.

It's hard for me to understand that some people are able to just switch on and off how much they care about people suffering. Maybe it's naive of me to even verbalize this, but I think it's the human in me that gets overwhelmed with the reality of how selective real support and allyship against racism and anti-semitism can be. A prime example is how Western European countries and the US treated Ukrainian asylum seekers in a very different manner than other refugees, because they're white. There is a law in Denmark that was passed in 2016 called the "jewelry law," where the Danish authorities can confiscate valuables from arriving refugees: cash, jewelry, and anything with value higher than 1,340 euro. This law was put in place when the Syrian asylum seekers were running away from war just like the Ukrainians. Yet, this law was lifted specially for Ukrainians coming into Denmark. Another example is the US making exemptions to cater to the influx of Ukrainian asylum seekers by lifting Title 42, which would give them access to seek asylum—not something offered to people coming from Latin American nations. To be clear, I think it's amazing to see international solidarity—that's a world I want to be part of!—but in many obvious ways it looks like the kindness and warm welcome isn't extended to everyone.

On an interpersonal level, I saw so many people on Instagram and who mean well follow the "trend" to help Ukraine when the country was first bombed, but a week later people were back at posting about their lives. I noticed nobody posting about the racially charged issue of African students in Ukraine being mistreated and in need of support as well.

Something that we've talked about before is that allyship is meant to be sustainable, which means broadening and examining how to be an anti-racist in your day-to-day. That means doing more than marching in the streets, reposting an easy-to-find graphic, or even donating money. It's being able to recognize minorities outside the struggle narrative that we are used to. Make sure you're reading things that expand your knowledge of a community and give money if you can. And again, this isn't about "saving" anyone, it should be something you do out of appreciation and love.

I come from Rwanda, and the two things people will bring up to me are the genocide against the Tutsi and the gorillas. These are very true and important things to speak about, but there's also so much more. I would expect my white friends to be curious about Rwanda in other ways: the music, the artists, the life there. Simply something that doesn't reduce our conversation to two things. Performative allyship is when you claim to support and care about a particular marginalized group but then that care doesn't reflect in your life. Maybe you have people around you that spew vile and dangerous things, for example. Your friendships don't reflect where you're at at the current stage in your life. It's like when I decided to quit drinking, there was a type of person I had to let go of. They were deep into the nightlife lifestyle—I never saw them during the day, only around a table dancing and drinking. Not to say I don't have friends that drink, most of my friends do, they just aren't about excessive drinking and partying, and they mostly reflect the things I care about. I know white people hate hearing this, and it's natural to hold on to what you know and are familiar with, but consider if you'd be able to invite your BIPOC friends around your other group of friends. Would that cause friction or be putting your BIPOC friends in an unsafe environment? Sometimes there's a difficult but necessary shedding that needs to be done. I'm not saying we can't have friends that think and see the world differently, but it really depends on the matter and we should agree on the same base in fundamental values of humanity—something that cannot be gambled with.

Active allyship works best when you make changes that feel genuine and align with the values you believe in; this applies to your friendships, environment, where you spend money, hang out, and so on. Active allyship is a lifestyle—just like when you decide to recycle and start to separate plastic and paper. It can't be something you wear as a badge and then take off when you're at home. You bring allyship into all of your spaces. You breathe it in and out and care about it all the time, not just when it will make you look or sound like a good person.

It's also very much about being able to see and support minorities without constantly supporting a trauma narrative. Meaning, you make sure to buy books by authors that are BIPOC or Jewish without it being about racism and antisemitism. There are Black authors that write about other things that aren't directly related to the struggles they face being Black. I find it wild that I have to say this, but a lot of the time when I do bring this up to people, I feel like the general response is like, "OMG, yes," but then you see all their book recommendations are about racism. It's funny to me that white people are so surprised by the suggestion that they learn about someone outside the struggle they experience.

Ultimately, only seeing someone in their struggles victimizes them and makes that pain a characterization of said people.

It doesn't equalize humanity to only see them in hurt. Also, it maintains the falsehood that BIPOC don't do anything else but work and talk about pain and struggle. I invite everyone to look at who invented the traffic light: Garrett Morgan in 1923. Or automatic elevator doors: Alexander Miles in 1887. The refrigerator truck: Frederick McKinley Jones in 1940. Carbon light bulb: Lewis Latimer in 1881, just to name a few crucial inventions we couldn't live without today.

I purposely included the dates because I want everyone to imagine the state of society in those times for Black people, and *still* they thrived. I mean it when I say that white allyship isn't meant to save us. I need white people to realize that you could make it easier for BIPOC simply by being more aware, informed, and a genuine ally. I've said this many times, but it's worth repeating that it's on white people to restore humanity robbed by white supremacy.

A Lifelong Journey

Yseult makes such an important point that we cannot just be allies when we are moved by pain and trauma. I think being an ally means seeing people in their full humanity and recognizing that we all share beauty and pain on the spectrum of human experience. If we're only focusing on the suffering of a group, we're dehumanizing them.

Being an ally is mostly an inner journey that requires time and dedication as we unpeel layers of conditioning. Some of us may even be unaware that there *are* layers to shed. Our society values productivity and expertise after we've completed the socially acceptable amount of higher education, but we have to approach allyship as lifelong students, because there is no graduation.

One of the first things we can take action on is considering where our time, money, and energy are going. Most of us have at least one of these resources to give.

Yseult and I did an initiative with *Kinswomen* in March 2021 where we encouraged our audience to buy from Black-owned brands for the month. I made as many purchases as possible from Black brands, from everyday items, like vitamins, to more permanent, like artwork. I ended up discovering so many BIPOC-owned companies that I'll support long-term. This initiative made me realize how much power we have with our dollars, and each purchase we make can have an impact.

One of my daily commitments to allyship is to do at least thirty minutes a day of reading or education by BIPOC authors and educators. I wrote this in my allyship mission statement, which I've shared on our site and on my Instagram, to keep me accountable. I highly recommend writing one for yourself. The most important thing about your mission statement is that it's realistic and doable, but also that it stretches you outside of your comfort zone. Whenever we've had white activists in our spaces and we've asked them how their allyship manifests on a daily basis, it's common that they fumble for an answer. This is something that we as white people should be asking ourselves, though. If it feels forced to work toward allyship daily, that's okay. It *will* take effort.

Maybe your goal this week is to have a conversation about something problematic your mother said about the Black Lives Matter movement, or to talk to your partner about why their comment about "not seeing color" is harmful. Begin with patience. Questions like "Why do you think that?" or "What did you mean by that?" are more productive than insulting, patronizing, or screaming through tears (been there) about how ignorant or racist you think they are. Normalize bringing up what's taboo.

Being an ally means that sometimes the person who must speak up is you. When it comes to bringing social justice into mostly white spaces, we can't assume that others are going to do it, or already have. It's also crucial to support the work that is already being done so that efforts are not duplicated. Be curious and be willing to listen to the underrepresented populations that you wish to be an ally to and take the lead from them. Do your own research, always, so that you're not burdening those you wish to be an ally to with questions and labor that you can find the answers to or do easily on your own.

Allyship is a muscle that gets stronger with time. Be accountable for your own actions first, and then bring your values to the spaces you occupy. I remember shaking and feeling red in the face going to HR and asking what their diversity efforts were. At the time, it felt so scary, like I would combust, or be fired just for bringing up issues of race. I'm sure that's how many white people who want to be allies feel—like we're powerless when it comes to even broaching the subject. But that's exactly what white supremacy is banking on: our silence and inaction.

Questions for Yseult

Q: When am I an ally to you?

I feel like you're an ally to me when I see that you are open and understanding to what I share. I feel supported as a Black person when I see that you see me as a person and not an artifact meant to teach you or help you be better. Anything that makes me feel like we've passed the stage of just exchanging for your growth. We connect on stuff that's not related to the work we do, like my weird and superniche interests, and we are able to vibe as people. Allyship in friendship is really caring about the other person as a human, not just on my experiences of being Black, and we have that in our friendship.

Also, I feel like you are an ally to me when I see that you care about other minorities' struggles or interests that aren't exclusively Black. Kind of like when you go on a dinner date and notice that your date is polite to waiters, and not just you because they are trying to impress you. I don't like or believe in exclusive allyship because all of it is interconnected.

Q: Have there been instances when I'm not?

There has been an instance where I felt unseen in my identity, yes! I've mentioned that because I want to be more observant in my Judaism for Shabbat, I've wanted to disconnect from work, starting every Friday night to Saturday sundown.

I had to say something a few times because you said you forgot, but I asked myself, if this was something that was related directly to my Blackness, would it have been accepted faster?

I started feeling really weird when I had to remind you a few times. My Jewishness is really important to me and is encompassed in who I am as a whole. I knew you understood that to an extent; we had shared Shabbat dinners and I've shared the things I've learned and know, but I felt resistance to respect my request. I felt as though you weren't acknowledging that part of me. I haven't had to remind you lately, but it is something I thought about and we had to have multiple conversations about.

It also reminds me that a lot of the time, I need to have this conscious attitude to make sure I express that I am more than my color of skin. I am more than the work we do, and I wasn't put here on earth to teach anyone specifically about race. I just happen to work in this space because when I think of my children and grandchildren, I want to know that I've tried to make things a bit better for them. As a Black woman, I have accepted that I need to remind the world that I am so much more, because white supremacy and anti-Blackness dehumanizes me and people that look like me. It strikes differently when you have to remind people close to you of that. These aren't questions white people have to experience, ever—they are seen and portrayed as human and complex beings.

I sometimes wonder, would a show like *Seinfeld* be possible with a cast of all Black people? It's one of my favorite shows, and its whole premise is a show about nothing and everything.

They are humans navigating the world and their friendships, and there's no dramatic plot or big lesson, but if it was an all-Black cast, they would have to portray everything that taps into a white person's mind and suits the white gaze to justify why the whole cast is Black. I hope that my children inherently feel worthy of leaning freely into all that they are without ever needing to remind themselves and others.

Q: What does it look like to be an ally when you're Black?

When it comes to things I love, I love to dive deep. I can't ensure that I am an ally to everyone, even if they are my friend, but when something comes to my attention and we have conversations about what they are experiencing, I make sure to integrate it into my advocacy and what I decide to learn about. I'm always trying to find intersectionality in these struggles and layered narratives, and I avoid any narrative that's black-and-white.

I know we are connected, all BIPOC, because the root of the struggles we share, even if they manifest differently, is white supremacy. I want to always be aware and admit when I haven't been inclusive of a group or that I didn't know about something in history. I'm always chasing the untold stories and alliances. For example, the truth is that most white people involved in the Civil Rights Movement were Jewish people. Martin Luther King Jr. had an ally in Rabbi Abraham Joshua Heschel, and together they marched, arm in arm, to Selma in 1965. I want to unpack and better understand how we have been stranded from allies and how we think we can exclude each other from our advocacy.

In America especially, there's been such an amazing and intersectional allyship between oppressed minorities, and I'm always trying to remind myself of that and share that through what we talk about in *Kinswomen*. We are interconnected—

we can't fight and eradicate white supremacy if we aren't inclusive of each other's struggles. For instance, there's no such scenario where Black people benefit but antisemitism isn't fought against, and antisemitism cannot overlook anti-Blackness that exists in Jewish spaces.

Questions for Hannah

Q: Do you have to be part of the community to be an ally?

I think that it's possible to be an aspiring ally without being inside or near the community that you want to be an ally to, but to really be an ally, the community would need to consider me one, as you've said previously.

For example, if I wanted to be an ally to the local Indigenous community, but I didn't know anyone locally, and I wasn't currently aware of the support they needed, the first step would be awareness. Often, we have no idea what less visible and underserved communities need or are experiencing because we're in our own bubbles. But with the Internet, the local library, and through conversation, there's really no excuse for ignorance. I've found through my involvement in one justice organization in my community that I'm exposed to so many other issues because they all intersect.

If I'm trying to be an ally to the Indigenous community, for example, I might try to learn from afar first, and then amplify the efforts that are already underway.

There are certainly those who exist within communities who are not allies, even if they try to be. I'm thinking about examples like mission trips to Africa and other volunteer initiatives in spaces that might be coming from a very patronizing, pro-assimilation mindset. I don't think it's allyship when I see white celebrities go to African countries and share pictures of themselves surrounded by Black children like they're the deity who's come to save them. The idea that we know what's best for a community we're not a part of is a very supremacist point of view, one that's often veiled in the concept of "charity." As white people, we must be conscious of our history of colonization and forced assimilation, and its violence and erasure.

Q: What were the moments you felt like you had to let go of something in order to be authentic in your allyship?

Quieting my ego in general has been a big part of me being an aspiring ally. It can be hard for me to concede that I've been wrong, like when you press me on something I said, and I get fragile and end up hurting you. I'm so used to defending myself—it's almost an automatic impulse, and I've recognized that in a lot of the conversations that we've had. I've realized how harmful my defensiveness can be in our conversations and relationship.

I've also had to accept that the more time I spend in this space, often, the less confidence I feel. Even though that sometimes feels unmooring, we've talked about how that's just part of the journey.

I've also had to let go of any kind of hierarchical allyship, like feeling better about myself by comparing myself to X or Y white person. Keeping a beginner's mindset is so important for me in this work, and in life in general. Also, understanding that this work can be really polarizing, and letting go of my desire to be liked by *all* people.

Q: How does your allyship manifest on a daily basis, in small ways?

Allyship for me starts at home, and at work. Am I being a good partner to my husband, or to you?

I can think of something that I've been working on the past few days, which is getting my apartment community to acknowledge Black Business Month and sharing local Black businesses with them. We get these monthly reminders about National Cookie Day or National Bike Day, and if they're going to send those out, why not acknowledge other "holidays" and months that actually affect people who live in their communities? I believe in going deep locally, because I have the most impact in the places where I spend the most time. As soon as we relocated from New York, I started going to the local city council meetings. From there, I met members of the local equality coalition, and have since joined the team. It's important to me to understand the issues that impact the people who live here. We've worked with the local police department on a de-escalation policy, as well as with local students. I'm also conscious of where I spend my money and try to buy from BIPOC business owners as much as possible. It doesn't take that much time to seek out Black-owned brands, but I have to be intentional about it until it's second nature. A lot of my allyship happens in the conversations that I have with friends or family. I also commit to my continuing education on the matter, but I don't necessarily consider that allyship, just a tool to help me on my allyship journey.

SIX
The Dos, Don'ts, and Hard Convos

Check In on Your Friends of Color—Or Don't?

We've experienced so much collective trauma as a society in the past few years, amplified by social media that exposes us to hourly horrors around the globe. For better or worse, we have much more exposure to national and global news than we did even ten years ago. This likely impacts our physical and mental health more than we realize. It's important to keep this in mind when it comes to our friends who experience racism and xenophobia—that they may be bombarded with seeing acts of violence committed against their community on a regular basis, thanks to the always-on nature of social media.

When traumatic things happen to specific marginalized groups, like the ongoing violence toward the Asian communities since Trump racialized the coronavirus in 2020, we must acknowledge their pain, and support our friends who are impacted. As in any friendship, we should be there for our friends during the highs *and* the lows. If we're white, it may feel awkward if we're not used to explicitly acknowledging race. I've questioned myself in these instances, wondering, for example, "Is it okay to check in on my Asian friends to see how they're doing? Will it seem performative, or will it retraumatize them?" These are important questions, but we also can't allow our discomfort to cloud our empathy. If your friend was experiencing something terrible that *wasn't* race-related, you'd check in, right? When Congregation Beth Israel Synagogue in Colleyville, Texas, was held hostage in January 2022, I felt seen and supported when both my Jewish *and* non-Jewish friends reached out to me. If you are genuinely friends and communicate regularly, reaching out to offer support shouldn't feel like an imposition—it's part of being a friend.

We don't bring up race with our friends, perhaps, because we imagine that it might mean that there's accountability required of us. We want our relationships to be a safe, egalitarian place, and sometimes that means we shy away from bringing up inequities that exist outside of them. We may even have to admit that our friendships may not be the safest places for our friends of color. I know that I can't always provide completely safe spaces for my friends of color. They might need to take breaks and set boundaries with me, and that's something that we as white friends should allow space for. Honoring that will make our friendships stronger in the long run.

If we've never talked about race in our interracial friendships, it will likely be uncomfortable territory, but that doesn't mean that it should be avoided. When broaching the topic, acknowledge that you haven't asked before, share why honestly, and be willing to admit if it's been due to your discomfort. Let your friend know why you're ready to discuss it *now*—and only if they themselves are willing and ready to do so. Then, you could start with a question like, "How do you need to be supported?" And most importantly, you listen.

★ ★ ★

When it comes to checking in, I feel the most comfortable when I initiate the conversation. I have a handful of friends with whom I feel comfortable asking for support in hard moments. I think check-ins are awkward when they come from people that you never talk to. That often feels voyeuristic. I think the first thing a white person needs to ask themselves before sending a check-in message is if they would ask a white friend that same potentially triggering thing, given the closeness and type of friendship. I am speaking from my own personal experiences about this. I have had this conversation with some Black friends who say they are totally open to check-ins, and others feel like me.

If there's a green light to reach out, it's super important that none of the information or feelings that were shared with you should be a subject of conversation with your fellow white friends. Like any sensitive conversation, white people need to realize that it shouldn't be casually laid out in front of other people without permission. This is so common and disturbing to me because it shows that our stories are just a tool to get an in, and they aren't taken as seriously as other intimate things that I share about. This is why I don't share personal information the same way with every white person.

What makes me feel more comfortable is when my white friends start a conversation with information and have done their own critical thinking. I shouldn't be the source of all your information, especially not during a moment of pain. I would like to normalize that white people who want to be allies to their friends of color should want to talk about things that expand beyond the BIPOC community. All of our conversations should not be centered on harm done on Black communities. These "isms" (racism, sexism, ableism) are interconnected and should be spoken about, otherwise it feels like I'm being singled out because of my identity, instead of wanting to have a productive conversation about making things better for everyone.

Another approach that I appreciate is to just ask the question "How are you?" casually, and not like you're checking in on me like I'm some hurt bird. Sometimes I want to share and sometimes I don't feel like it, depending on the person and moment. Even with Hannah, I don't always want to share how I'm feeling, and I'll also tell her if I'm not ready to speak on something that happened in the media. We have to normalize a healthy cycle of grief and leave space for BIPOC, Jewish people, and other marginalized communities to take as much time as they need to process. Asking how someone is doing isn't supposed to be your turn to say what you think and feel; it's to make sure that you're nurturing space as a friend to talk about everything.

Hannah and I are new friends. We haven't known each other for very long yet, but we've been able to connect in a lot of ways that are meaningful. Since we are still growing and getting to discover parts of each other, I know that there needs to be space given for grace and patience. For me, that means when she does check in, I have had to take the time to verbalize what I felt good about and what I didn't. I see this as a healthy way to build boundaries to make our friendship stronger. I think these boundaries are crucial to verbalize and accept, especially in moments when something highly emotional is happening between us and outside us. That's my way of going about this, but I also realize that whiteness has a level of entitlement that creeps in on our white friends without knowing. This sense of entitlement when checking in can be super draining for me and I imagine for other BIPOC who experience it.

I set realistic expectations for myself in these moments; that's why I keep in mind that when I do accept my friends checking in, that I'm ready to also share. At the end of the day, checking in with your friends should be natural, and it should be done from a place of love and compassion. Putting your own ego aside is the best way.

That's my way of going about this, but I also realize everyone has their own boundaries and ways of interacting within friendships.

The White Lens and Non-White Friends

Now that we've outlined what the white lens is in a previous chapter, it's important to be conscious of how we as white people can bring that lens into our friendships. When Yseult found out that I loved the 2000s television show *Gilmore Girls*, since I'd often post memes to social media, she sent me a link to a now-defunct Tumblr page by Rahawa Haile called "gilmoreblacks," a visual anthology of every Black cast member on the show since the pilot. The page showed that almost every single Black actor was an extra with no name or spoken lines. At first, I was slightly annoyed when she sent me the link, thinking, "Can't I just have this?!" But, despite my wanting to defend it, she was right! Seven seasons, plus a Netflix reboot, and only one Black recurring character.

Growing up watching the show in the early 2000s and then later as an adult, my white lens didn't see what Haile, Yseult, and so many other viewers of color likely saw. Haile told *Nylon* in 2016: "The purpose of *Gilmore Girls* isn't to celebrate diversity; it never was. The issue isn't that the show needs more diversity. It's that the show's idea of diversity reduces minorities to stereotypes or treats them as props."[24] She's right. And Yseult wasn't trying to steal my joy; she was pointing out that I need to be willing to be critical of what I love.

Now I can't watch the show the same way—its overwhelming whiteness and other problematic themes make it difficult

---

24   https://www.nylon.com/articles/black-actors-on-gilmore-girls.

for me to watch mindlessly like I used to. I share this to point out that what we love and normalize may be things that our non-white friends see as exclusionary, awkward, and might even be unsafe for them—things like country music concerts, cross-country road trips, or theme parties that have been planned by and for white people without considering the identities, safety, or sensitivities of those outside of whiteness. What we as white people may view as welcoming are not circumstances that are universally welcoming to everyone in return.

In June 2020, Rachel Berry, a Black country music fan from New Jersey, wrote about this experience gap on Instagram, saying that she looks up a town's racist history before considering going to a show there, and though she loves going to festivals and fairs, she often feels uneasy seeing Confederate flags waving from people's trucks. She wrote, "I find myself almost wishing I was invisible so I could walk through the crowd without being seen or noticed."[25]

If we are white, these may not be experiences we'd anticipate or consider beforehand, but for the physical and psychological safety of our friends of color, they must be. Seeing Confederate flags waved proudly is disturbing for me, too, but the threat and implication is not the same for me as it is for Rachel, since I walk around in a white body. I'm not saying events like these need to be avoided if you're inviting friends of color or attending with them, just considered carefully, with everyone's consent up-front, and even a plan of action for worst-case scenarios.

As white people, we have to be conscious about the environments we're bringing our friends of color into. If those group settings are mostly or completely white, I believe that our BIPOC friends should be given a heads-up. We should prepare our friends in advance so that they have the choice to opt out.

---

25   https://www.goodmorningamerica.com/culture/story/womans-powerful-post-black-country-music-fan-viral-71153147.

While it might be awkward to point out the racial makeup of an upcoming gathering—since in doing so, we'd have to acknowledge the topic of race in the first place—getting consent from our friends before we bring them into situations where they may feel the glaring spotlight of being an "only" is a habit that aspiring allies should adopt. This is something that I haven't always done because I felt that same discomfort about bringing it up.

While each friendship has individual needs that will evolve over time, and there is no prescription for an interracial friendship, friendships across race often require additional sensitivity. Some of you might argue that taking our friends' race into account minimizes them to just one aspect of their identity. But what I'm advocating for is acknowledging the full spectrum of our friends' identities and considering how those different aspects impact the way they interact with the world, and the way the world interacts with them.

Dos & Don'ts

I know it's tempting to create a written list of things that are easy to check off for your own growth, but I don't want anyone to think it's that simple when it comes to cross-racial friendships. We are so diverse as people. Our preferences and pressure points from one person to the next won't be the same. The idea of using a checklist as a way to interact with your friends of color isn't fair to our personal stories. That said, here are some "dos" based on my own personal experiences that I think are helpful to share.

My first "do" for white people has to do with their overall mindset and reason for wanting to do anti-racism work: be a decent human. Make sure you're treating your friends who happen to be people of color the same way you would any other friend of yours who is white. There's no clear map for driving the road to allyship because my asks aren't the same as another Black person's, but all interactions should come from a place of love and actual affection for your friend.

Another "do" is to accept that whether the friendship or intimate relationship is two years old or twenty, white people need to remember that they can still make mistakes and need to be able to hear us when we bring up something that's harmful. The longevity of a relationship does not make us immune to your harm. I have experienced moments where white people assumed that because we were close that I would overlook their behavior and not be "caught in my feelings," just because we know each other. If I say something felt wrong and I want to talk about it, because we are friends that should mean that it's easier to create a space to address things.

A big "don't" is to think that apologies are the end of being called in on something. So many people that mess up in public are quick to say sorry, but three months later find themselves in some similar mess. I would suggest white people apologize, but also use the moment as an opportunity to learn from their mistake. Understand where your friend's sentiment came from and how you can make sure to avoid the same type of incident in the future. Otherwise, it's exhausting to be around someone who is more likely to trigger me again without taking accountability for their actions. Storms give birth to flowers, so the interpersonal storms that happen between friends should be an opportunity for growth.

Don't make your friendship with your BIPOC or Jewish friends exclusively about their identities. We exist outside of our race and the trauma caused by white supremacy. Being able to be friends is getting to know someone in *all* that they are. I don't want to talk about race stuff all the time. I want to be able to be the artist I am and engage in other interests and joys. These things can coexist. It is especially important for white people that are trying to be allies to understand because they tend to focus exclusively on talking about race in a traumatic way, when they want to show that they care. Humanizing someone is also making sure that you accept all the versions that they want to offer you.

Don't center yourself. I think it's normal, because as humans we frame things in how we relate to them. But it hits differently when we are speaking on race because there's pain and experiences that cannot equate to whatever experience a white person has to compare it to. Also, as a friend, you should be able to make space without making it about you. Otherwise it comes off as a battle of "trauma Olympics" and that's not why BIPOC share things or call you in. I think it's valid to share your life experiences and pain outside of when your BIPOC friends share theirs, as that's all part of building friendships.

A BIG DON'T, and my biggest pet peeve, is when I suddenly become Google for people on what is racist. I don't want to be that person because it's not a simple yes or no question. It's something I would have to spend time thinking and speaking about, which can be emotionally and mentally exhausting.

As a good rule of thumb is that if you have to ask, it's probably something racist. There are a lot of resources online and in books that can be referenced instead of relying on me to educate you.

The list of dos and don'ts will expand depending on your individual friends, but I think that the overall goal is to remember how much you care for them and why you are close. This should be guided by reconciliation and love. If it doesn't work out and a BIPOC friend decides to end a friendship because they don't feel seen and understood, that's okay, too, and should be read as a form of self-preservation and not just rejection.

Like Yseult said, every friendship has different rules, most of them unspoken. Our friendships are nuanced and layered. But whether your interracial friendship is budding or long-term, setting boundaries and expectations is a form of respect and protects the integrity of the relationship. The boundaries Yseult and I have set didn't happen right away—they took time as we were getting to know each other. Now, several years into our friendship, I know not to talk to her about work on Shabbat, but this was a boundary I kept forgetting (i.e. didn't respect) until she had to tell me several times. Perhaps because I wasn't used to explicit, verbal boundaries in friendships, I kept "forgetting," at great expense to Yseult and our relationship. In interracial friendships, boundaries couldn't be more important to honor.

I remember meeting up with Yseult for the first time, just her and me, after we'd decided to start the podcast together. Up until that point, we'd only interacted in the context of our monthly conversations between women of color and white women in my living room. Over matcha and tea, we shared our family histories, our wounds, our motivations, and our fears to see if we could connect on a more intimate level. That conversation was a bridge from being acquaintances to friends.

Despite growing up in different parts of the world and having different identities, we found the threads that connected us. From a spiritual level, I know she is in my life for a purpose that's even beyond my comprehension.

I've found that one of the joys of making new friends later in life is that we can be more intentional about who we want in our lives and what we expect from them, whereas long-term friendships are often rooted in where we were located (school, theater camp, work), and can become stagnant and resistant to change.

Being able to share my full self is something I value so highly in friendships. As I've grown in my allyship, and continued my work with *Kinswomen*, some of my friendships have fallen away. I've recognized that my evolution has come with consequences, and that's okay. Because of the openness and vulnerability shared, some of my deepest friendships are those that started during our living room conversations just a few years ago. Those relationships are a gift, and they motivate me to be a better ally and person—like the best friendships should do.

Sitting in the Sh*t

I'm always trying to strike the right balance and aim for integrity when it comes to listening and responding during hard conversations. I can be overly defensive because I'm haunted by all the times I shut up and put up with being treated badly. And I can be silent because I'm haunted by the things that I've said in the heat of the moment and later regretted. Most of us are not equipped or taught how to have hard conversations, especially not those about race. Confrontation can make us either fight, flight, or freeze. Rarely do we process the discomfort and listen—and that's how the transformation and healing can happen.

Sadly, we (white people) typically meet any race-related tension brought to our attention by our BIPOC or white friends with vehement denial. Common responses? "I don't have a racist bone in my body!" or "That wasn't my intention!" or "I wasn't even considering race when I said/did that!" I've both said or heard all of these. The discomfort we feel often manifests as defensiveness and centering our own feelings, two toxic responses that will do us no good. Even if I've felt justified at the time, I always regret responding in this way after the fact. When it comes to conversations about race and racism, instead of reacting or responding immediately, we as white people need practice sitting in the discomfort and processing what is being said.

If a BIPOC friend or colleague tells you that something you said or did was problematic, at first it won't feel like what it is: a gift. What happens in the space between the moment in question being brought to your attention and realizing this truth will make all the difference in your interracial relationships.

Having hard conversations about race will take practice. But to avoid causing potential harm to your friends of color with denial and defensiveness, I suggest first bringing awareness to where you've been evading important conversations elsewhere in your life, and building up your capacity for sitting in their truth and discomfort. What needs to be voiced when it comes to weighty topics like sex, money, self-worth, or trauma? Keep in mind these could be conversations that you should simply be having with yourself.

I used to put off the monthly finance meetings that my husband initiated because I felt so much stress, shame, and anxiety. I wanted to avoid the uncomfortable feelings that came up for me around money. With more awareness, I realized that I had a lot of healing to do around scarcity, security, and self-worth. My husband wanted to have these meetings to connect as partners about our finances and future, not to make me feel terrible. I came to realize that my response and my healing was my responsibility, not his—and that started with sitting in the uncomfortable muck of my feelings. The more I did that, the less intense the feelings became, and the less I avoided our meetings.

Even telling my hairdresser (kindly) that I didn't like the haircut that she gave me was difficult, but if I'm not willing to sit in discomfort over my hair, how can I sit in discomfort when it comes to race? You, too, may want to avoid discomfort completely. But ask yourself: Am I willing to let discomfort be the barrier between me and deeper relationships, my healing, and... better haircuts? Whether we're the ones who need to speak up or the ones who must listen, there are likely countless conversations that we should be having that we're too scared to broach.

Learning To Listen

In cross-racial dialogues, however, we should *always* defer to those who experience racism. Depending on how you identify, you may have varying degrees of familiarity with deferment. If you identify as white but also as a woman, you might feel exasperated at being asked to defer to people of color—perhaps you feel like you've experienced a lifetime of having to cede the floor to white men. As a white millennial woman raised on "Girl Power!" feminism, I've been taught by our culture to use my voice as an act of resistance. That might seem contradictory to the message here, but when it comes to matters of race, we need to do less talking and more listening. It's not about being silenced—it's acknowledging that our words can be (and have been) harmful, so we must be mindful. The words of white people have created so much inequity and pain. Let's not add to that legacy. When it comes to race, the more time spent listening, the greater the impact our words will have when we do lend our voices.

Listening deeply must be rooted in a genuine desire to understand what we don't know. And it may be uncomfortable as white people to admit that there is *so much* we don't know—about race, about our history, about how the non-white people in our lives actually feel about us. Many of us will nobly say that we have a desire to bridge the gaps, build trust, and create a more equitable future. But the work that it'll take to get there will happen outside of our comfort zones. And when we're outside of them, our pride, our resistance, and our denial won't want to listen, as if the issues are with everyone but us.

In the process of writing this book, my own denial, discomfort, and refusal have come to the surface. In one instance, my desire for rightness emerged over a single word that Yseult objected to—and I was willing to go to battle for it. In the context of writing about how we as white people aren't simply racist or not, I used the word "binary." Yseult made a comment that the word felt co-opted from the queer community. Irked, I responded that the word had many applications. The conversation escalated as I continued to argue my point. In hindsight, I was

143

more concerned with the Webster definition of this word and being "right" than listening to Yseult.

I responded emotionally as if she was questioning me, my character, and my intelligence, rather than my use of a single word. The argument also came near the end of writing the first draft of this book, after she'd challenged many other portions of my writing, so, feeling weary, I pushed back against this particular criticism. However, all of her earlier objections and suggestions were not only fair, they were generous. Gifts. She's pushed me to think more deeply about my own responsibility; she's helped me as a writer and a human—and I can imagine that it was also emotionally exhausting for her to read pages and pages of my writing and feel triggered or hurt by my words.

Was it easy to hear that certain parts of my writing struck her as problematic throughout the course of cowriting this book? Not at all. At times, I responded with defensiveness when I should have simply listened. Knowing that emotions can come up when it comes to these conversations, I could have asked for some time to take her comments in. With a bit of space, I would have recognized that Yseult wanted to be heard and was calling me in to be better, not chastising me as a poor writer, friend, and ally—which is how my ego wanted to see it. It's in our unwillingness to listen where we risk causing further harm to our friend and to the relationship.

In a situation where we're called in, what should we do? Here are some guidelines:

- First, express appreciation to your friend for bringing the issue to your attention. It's a sign of trust if your friend felt comfortable enough to speak up.

- If you're feeling defensive or emotional, ask for some time to take in what they said.

- Apologize if you reacted with anger or defensiveness. Own up to your discomfort. Refrain from centering your own feelings.

- Focus on the impact you had on your friend over your intention.

- Share what you've learned from the exchange, and how you'll avoid similar behavior in the future.

- Take time to reflect.

- Be willing to give your friend space if they need it.

These aren't guidelines that I've adhered to perfectly by any means, but they're what I aim for.

Fess Up to Your Mess-Ups

I've spoken with other white, aspiring ally friends who've felt crushed by shame after messing up with their friends of color. After a rupture, or even a minor mistake, they convinced themselves that there was no hope left for them as allies. I can understand the feeling, because I've felt that way, too. The shame of our actions not aligning with our values can feel so humiliating that we decide to just give up on our allyship journey. It's important to remember, in having conversations about race, that we will mess up. Apologies and repair will be required, and we must use what we learned from the experience to further our progress in this work.

One white woman that I met in a social justice group shared with me that she was recently divorced from her husband, who was Black. The marriage ended because he didn't feel supported in his Blackness in their partnership. She'd been involved in activism during their relationship, and after the divorce, she struggled with what it meant to be an ally after feeling like she'd let down the one person she most wanted to be an ally to. Her biggest fear as a white woman had manifested, and it made her question her role in allyship. After a period of confusion, she began to reflect on what led to the demise of her marriage and used the experience to continue to educate herself on being a better ally. She let the experience inform what she could do better, and she didn't use the shame as an excuse to stop learning.

After self-reflection, a sincere apology can make all the difference in repairing a friendship, and it's no different when the fracture is race-related. When we've caused harm and it's been brought to our attention, our responsibility is to apologize and make amends. White pride has gotten in the way of progress for too long. Let's be humble enough to say *enough* and be willing to admit that we got it wrong.

White supremacy has a lot to apologize for. On a global scale, there are few examples of accountability. During Prince William and Duchess Kate's royal tour of the Caribbean in March 2022, for example, they were met with protests in Belize, Jamaica, and the Bahamas, with protestors calling for reparations and a formal apology for the colonization and slave trade that made Britain wealthy and the Caribbean countries poor. At a dinner in Jamaica, Prince William said, "I want to express my profound sorrow. Slavery was abhorrent and it should never have happened."[26] Advocates and leaders from those Caribbean countries condemned William for stopping short of offering a formal apology and plan for reparations.

On a societal scale and in our personal relationships, an apology is the first step toward repair and restoration. Perhaps we refuse to apologize not only because of the difficulty in admitting that we were wrong, but because an apology acknowledges that we must be better. "Better" might require abolishing institutions

---

26 https://www.nytimes.com/2022/03/25/world/americas/royal-couple-caribbean-visit.html.

and ways of operating that cater to white comfort and security, and a reimagining of who we are.

As white people, having conversations about race will reveal our deepest insecurities and challenge who we believe ourselves to be. We need to listen and welcome that challenge.

SEVEN

The Realities of Interracial Friendships and Relationships

My first experience seeing an interracial relationship up close is from my childhood. My parents have been married for a very long time—twenty-plus years. My father is a Belgian white man and my mother is a Burundian and Rwandan Black woman. They met young in Bujumbura, an African city in Burundi, the country where my brother Ricky and I were both born. Because it's shaped like a human heart, some call Burundi the heart of the continent. Small details like that create a romantic setup for a modern-day love story.

My father had decided he wanted to travel to Africa and live there for a few years. He was young, and I think he was doing some late '80s–style soul-searching. What I admire is that he sought schooling first, so that he didn't arrive in Africa with his only qualifications being white and privileged. (Strong side-eye to random white kids, barely eighteen, deciding to go "save Africans" with nothing but positive vibes in their pockets, and their only qualification a strong, delusional, G-d-like complex, but I digress.) Soon after getting a veterinary degree at the Institute of Veterinary Medicine of Antwerp, diploma in hand, he booked a ticket and moved to Burundi, finding work at a chicken farm owned by religious nuns in the countryside. Both my parents, jokingly, like to share that he wasn't great at working with animals! My father later explained that it wasn't a passionate choice but rather something that felt practical.

For the next few years, he was busy working at the farm, riding on the infamous red dirt roads of the region on his vintage Yamaha XT350, sporting ripped jeans and his superlong hair, cruising through the thousands of hills of Burundi and beyond. My parents first met where my mother worked. She was the first person that greeted guests at the Hotel Lac Tanganyika that sits just on the border of Lake Tanganyika. It's one the biggest lakes in the world and is the continuation of the Nile River up north of the continent, ending in the Burundi region. It's spectacular how it looks like a beach. People hang out on the sand, the water is fresh, and legend says the oldest and largest crocodile in the world, named Gustave, lives in the lake. At least that's the story I grew up hearing. My dad said that the first time he met my mother she was in her serious work outfit, and he felt like she was a square. She didn't pay him any mind because she was working, but they ran into each other again—this time on the beach in normal clothes, and my dad says that she looked so different. That night is when they both noticed each other, decided to hang out, and the rest is history.

The day my parents got married, they celebrated by sitting on the Yamaha, with a few of their friends, sipping on some Fanta and Coca-Cola. Both of my parents had a pretty diverse group of friends. I've seen some pictures from their wedding day, and they looked so young and beautiful with their friends. My mother was wearing a cute green dress, the type Congolese women wear with gold patches on it, and a green, supersimply tied headpiece. My dad wore a purple suit with a flower motif on his tie. They both looked so cool and at ease, surrounded by their friends in Bujumbura. A true vision, something that growing up I idolized, and that many around us idolized about them as well.

I feel protective of their story, because I don't want it to be tarnished by preconceived negative ideas, or the romanticization of their union, like they were some '90s Benetton ad. Their relationship was based on genuine affection, not to "prove the world has solved racism" or to be anything more than two young people finding love and starting a life together. But there are three crucial elements of their story that I think are helpful to consider when it comes to interracial relationships.

First, I want to mention the age aspect. I always want people to know that they were the same age, meaning it wasn't a power play—killing off a potential story line of the old colonial dude dealing with his midlife crisis by finding a young African girl to start all over with.

Then, location: I need people to know that my father met my mother in her home country. My mother was working and living independently when they met. She wasn't an African girl who had ended up an immigrant in Europe and found a white dude to marry—she was living her life and loved being in Burundi. She had grown up there, and my grandmother and family were there as well. She met my father when she was going about her life.

I despise the narrowed, white-gaze narratives of minorities leaving their home country because of it being "better in Europe/America," like their lives prior to living in the West are erased or were only filled with horrific events and terrible conditions—as if their birth land isn't worth remembering. But can a tree ever completely separate itself from its roots, no matter how tall it becomes?

They had a life in Burundi that has contributed to who they are—the foods they love, the music, the smells, the people and friends they have. Humans have historically been nomads of this world. But when we see a white person move into a Brown, Asian, or Black country, it's romanticized as a story of discovery and native-saving. White people in these foreign countries still experience an immense sense of white privilege—they need to do even less to get much more. Their egos are filled with the sense of being a savior or that they are special. Also, we ignore all the Westerners who move to Africa and Asia because there is good business to be made. Like all immigrants, they move to these countries to get a better life.

Last thing I'd like to share is that my father wasn't there to feed into a white colonialist rhetoric. He genuinely wanted to live in Burundi and brought a real skill to his new home. One extreme example of how this white colonialist mindset can gravely affect a community in a Black, Brown, or Asian country is the situation caused by Renee Bach. A white woman from Virginia, she had been pumped up by the church narrative of saving African babies, and without any skills or training decided to open a makeshift hospital in Uganda.

She wore a white coat and pretended to know how to treat the children that were brought by their families for care. They called her "the white doctor." It was later revealed that she barely finished high school and believed she was supposedly called by G-d to save these babies. The only diploma this girl had was a PhD in white saviorism. Her impact was horrific; she left a community that trusted her to deal with the health of their children in a worse state than when she arrived, because she wanted to feel special. But to do something this horrible— who do you pray to? After being found out, she ran back to the US to her family, leaving a whole community hurt and grieving the loss of their babies. Though a few families have sued her, they have not gotten justice, and she gets to go back to her "real life" without any consequences for her actions. I'm sure she misses feeling like a white savior.

What troubles me the most about this whole situation is that she could've never done that in her own home country, but felt like Africa was a playground where she could play make-believe doctor with people who trusted her. She ended up having children that are mixed race, Black and white. I am curious about the conversation she will one day have when they are old enough to realize how insane and racist her behavior was. I DIGRESS.

Getting back to interracial relationships, whether they're intimate or platonic, they are used to justify that racism has been abolished. I can't tell you how many commercials and advertisements I saw growing up feeding into that lie. I have to admit, in the earlier years of my life, I believed if people were able to love each other and have babies, or be best friends, we were in a post-racial era. I soon realized, however, that a post-racist era would require so much more than that. Obviously as human beings, we naturally want to connect with one another, and people will mix to a certain extent. It's hard to fight the nature of who we are as humans. While it's wonderful seeing people love each other in different ways, there's still work we need to do, more we must speak on, laws we need to abolish. There are still injustices that affect minority groups, even if mixed babies are being born and interracial friendships are being made. My wish is that the energy that we carry to marry and have interracial friendships goes toward doing more, and not resting on the myth of a post-racial society.

When I first started dating, the pool of people around me was mostly white. I remember early on in my dating life, my mother told me, "Listen, try to date a Black person." I was young and didn't have the perspective I have now, which made me super confused as to what she was saying. I mean, she was married to my father, a white man! Why would she say that to me? Wasn't she open-minded? Could I bring only Black people back home? It made no sense to me at the time. Fast-forward to actually dating white people, and now I understand what she meant. I knew that my parents had experienced their own tribulations from my father's family when they got together, but I thought, "I'm from the new generation, that stuff is dead, and my partner's parents will be cool and accepting." There are just certain things you have to experience to understand. My mother wasn't trying to block me in my dating escapades, but rather didn't want me to experience the hardships she had to go through. I also quickly understood that not everyone was like my dad, because he was willing to cut people that didn't accept us from his life. That's the type of real-life love you want to see your partner demonstrate.

That being said, I would like to share some tips I learned from dating white people. First, it's a red flag when they have no friends that are Black or POC (or only have the one token Black/BIPOC friend). It doesn't mean that they should immediately be swiped left, but it means that you should brace yourself for uncomfortable comments and conversations. I would also try to figure out if they are at least interested in or familiar with anything other than their own culture and people— travel, reading, and overall general knowledge. I have been with people who were POC who knew nothing about my culture and Blackness, but their overall attitude was respectful, and it didn't feel objectifying. I think that was due to the fact that they were POC and understood how it feels to be "other," especially in a romantic relationship.

Another tip is to engage in casual conversation to test the waters. People reveal a lot about themselves in normal conversations. And I'm protecting myself, because I don't have to share a personal story, especially if it's still raw and I haven't processed it and it could possibly be retraumatizing depending on how they respond. I am an intense person, I have come to accept that, so my tolerance is as thin as the air I gasp when white people say some dumb shit.

One time I tried this out to gauge a person I was getting to know—they were white, from France, and we actually had a lot in common. They knew my country's overall history, and they had Black friends that I personally found cool and funny. I was still trying to figure out if my date would be a ride or die when something weird came up.

We were watching a movie and the scene was about a cop stopping a Black couple on the road for no reason. The cop proceeded to insinuate that the luxurious car they were driving was stolen. I mean, it was textbook racist stuff. The cop pushed around the husband and "searched" the wife by sexually assaulting her in front of the husband. I was appalled but not surprised by the situation. I said, "Oh my G-d, that's disgusting," and my voice was kind of emotional. I turned to my date, waiting for "Oh yeah, that's so racist." He said nothing, even shrugged his shoulders like a kid.

I sat there thinking, *Damn, I kinda liked him*. I thought, *Girl, you out here putting makeup on to look like a snack. Why don't you push and give him a chance to make it better?* I continued, "Don't you think there's a problem there?"

He looked at me and said, "Oh, I don't know."

That conversation told me the kind of person I was dealing with. I mean, I think he felt weird and uncomfortable, and probably had no idea how to address it. Mentally, I swiped left on him and knew it wasn't going to be a thing. I'll be a hundred percent though—your girl still spent the night, because things are weird like that. I know it's some weak shit, but I'm way more conscious now than I was then. I have forgiven myself.

I realized in more mature relationships that the pain from interracial dating isn't just from their families and friends. The partner can be the cause of hurt, too. That wasn't something I considered, as I hadn't witnessed that with my parents. But I had to make peace that the way racism showed up in my parents' union isn't the only way it manifests. Sometimes it comes from the very person you took the time to select to be the one you love. It hurts like a dart straight to the heart when this happens. I've been with people where I thought it would be us against the world, but sometimes the hurt is entangled with the love you feel for the person.

Listen, I have to be honest—there's no way to really explain how confusing that feeling is. When your partner is harmful in some way, they also tend to think that you should give them more time and understanding than you would everyone else. For me, the harm done by a partner hurts the most because of two things: First, I feel as if I failed the screening process. The longer you're in the relationship, the more confusing it becomes that you didn't spot it before. Second, you've made yourself open and vulnerable. The hurt hits hard and feels like a betrayal. I realized in those moments that white supremacy was so insidious and embedded in people's minds so deeply that they had a hard time even seeing it until it was too late. I would look at this person, like, *I love you, how can you!* It's layered and so complex because of the love you have for them. In these moments I have thought that sometimes love is just not enough, depending on the person and situation. I mean, it's a lot to handle.

But then you remember they are amazing and you love them, and it's like you're forced to decide to hold this person's hand while you are emotionally overwhelmed by the pain they are causing. You want to run. I understand how weird and complex this all is. I don't have a clear answer, but I do know as a Black woman, your heart has to be preserved, and relationships with white people have to be one of those "case by case" things. *Is it worth it? Can we work on this?* I had to let go of shame from the idea that it was my fault I didn't choose the "perfect" person. I have learned to prioritize my mental and heart health. I don't ever want to forget that I need space for peace, especially when I'm with someone that I love. I want to be able to be honest in my relationships, because couples ideally should be like teams.

My truth is also that the most pain I have experienced has come from white people that were the closest to me, either through friendships, romantic partners, or family on my father's white side. It's hard when you have given these people the proximity and emotional attachment and then they say or do something that's racist. The impact of their actions is greater than if it was from a stranger or the society we live in. I have always been cautious in choosing the friends I have in my life. I let my heart guide me, but my brain also interjects to make sure I ask questions or engage in conversations to know where a new friend stands.

I realize it may sound harsh to imagine that I go through almost an interview process before I'll be friends with someone, but I want to be able to share and indulge in who I am: a woman, queer, and also African and Black. In the end, I've become comfortable taking these extra steps if it means peace and good vibes, and that my Blackness and the topics related to it aren't something I need to keep away from people.

The joys and tribulations of being a Black woman in an overwhelmingly white environment is a whole mood that deserves time for conversation. Similar to when women come together and speak about being women: whether it's in motherhood, work culture, or simply existing in the world, it's nice when you have girl time to dish on the hardships and know that others know exactly what you are talking about and can validate your experiences.

At the end of the day, with those that we love the most, we want to feel held and supported through ups and downs. Being a BIPOC, you shouldn't have to hold back on a chunk of your experience to avoid shaking the table. I want to smash the table and shake it all up because it's together that things can feel a little less horrible. So, the real takeaway is that it's not about having the right answer or even "saving" your friend, but learning how to be there and giving space and legitimacy to what your close friend is expressing.

The Responsibilities of White Partners

Growing up, I watched my Jewish father and my Catholic mother try to blend their religions and traditions in our home. My father, who was less devout than my mother, let Catholicism reign, and so we went to church and Sunday school every week and tolerated confession. Though we'd celebrate Passover and go to our Jewish cousins' bat mitzvahs, Judaism was treated as secondary in our home. Being Jewish is a culture just as much as it is a religion, but besides my dad's side of the family, we didn't have a lot of Jewish people around us to nurture it. Also, my dad loves Christmas. He's a proud Jew, but each December, he wears a Santa hat unironically. Moving to New York, a city of Jewish people, and going on Birthright, the pilgrimage to Israel for Jewish youth, helped strengthen my relationship to my culture. After that trip to Israel, where there was not-so-subtle pressure to pair off and continue the race, I left certain that I'd end up with a Jewish guy.

Instead, I met my husband, and we fell quickly in love. It was my first significant interracial relationship. Now that we're married and we're creating our own family, I think often about how we integrate our own cultures, and how easy it can be for one person's identity to subsume parts of the other's if one is more prevalent, or if there is pressure to assimilate. Most importantly, I do not want my husband to feel like we have to submit to whiteness in our home just because whiteness is dominant outside of our home. I want him (and our future children) to know and feel that Blackness is honored and not secondary to whiteness, ever. At our wedding ceremony, we both broke the glass in the Jewish tradition and jumped the broom to honor the African American one. We intend to make that inclusive spirit part of our legacy as a couple.

When we first got together almost a decade ago, I entered into our relationship with a naivete that I'm not proud of. My thinking was: he's Black, I'm white…and we'll live happily ever after. I lived my life up until that point with a general sense of safety, security, and trust in the law enforcement and institutions intended to protect me and other white people. I also enjoyed the benefit of presumed innocence and knew that because I appeared nonthreatening—I'm a petite white woman—that I'd likely be able to get out of whatever trouble I got myself into. My approach in life was: "Better to beg for forgiveness than ask for permission." I didn't recognize at the time that those viewpoints were steeped in white privilege, and that they were the complete inverse of my husband's approach to the world. Color blindness had made me blind to those truths.

While I could feel eyes on us in public in a way that I never did with white partners, at first I didn't think much about Dave and me being different races. He didn't really bring it up either. But eventually, the differences in the way we responded to the world around us and how it responded back became clear, even if we weren't voicing them.

In our early days of dating, my husband and I were taking a walk through the West Village, and I noticed that a gate was open to a courtyard that was usually closed. When I suggested that we explore and headed toward the gate, he kindly but firmly refused, staying a good distance away on the sidewalk. In that moment, I saw in his stance that his "exploring" could be interpreted as trespassing, a risk he wasn't going to take. I, on the other hand, could've safely poked around, knowing that I'd be taken for a resident or guest, not a threat. That was one of my first wake-up calls. I felt embarrassed and ashamed for not considering his safety and kicked myself for being so naive and so *white*. It wasn't enough just to love him—I had to wake up to what I'd chosen not to see to be the best possible partner to him.

I noticed the Uber drivers who would not acknowledge him, or people who'd think he was the bouncer if we were standing outside of a bar. These moments were painful to witness, but for my husband, they were routine, and he didn't like to harp on them. That would add to my rage, knowing that this racism was so common as to be anticipated. My outrage was not appreciated by Dave, however. It only brought more attention to him in those situations, and to me as the white woman who was just beginning to see the truth. At first, I was only seeing these interactions on the surface level, as if racism was the result of individual prejudices. But over time and with education, I started to see these interactions as being supported by a deep, intentional structure of racism.

My husband takes what seems like hundreds of measures a day to be perceived as nonthreatening as possible. On his daily runs, he makes sure to take the same route. He figures that if he runs past the same windows regularly, people will assume he's a resident in our neighborhood, and will be less likely to react in ways that could put him in danger. That's just one measure for one moment in his day. (If only white people took even a *fraction* of those measures to make people of color feel more comfortable!) He feels the pressure to both disprove the stereotypes that exist about Black men and the pressure to not live in opposition to what white people might assume about him.

This kind of overthinking about everything takes a toll on him. This is another privilege that I have—the absence of mental energy about how my race is perceived by the white majority. Though I'm constantly aware of my vulnerability as a woman living in rape culture, I think white supremacy is even more insidious, though it goes hand-in-hand with patriarchy. The stress of living in survival mode takes an emotional and mental toll that cannot be underestimated. The burden, instead, should be on white people, or any majority wielding power, to stop inflicting the suffering.

Before you say that if a Black man ran past your window you wouldn't think twice as a white person: please don't. There are too many examples in our recent history that reinforce the reality that white reactions can lead to the death of people of color. Even if we imagine that we're exempt from the convenience of stereotypes, we all have reflexive implicit biases that can be truly dangerous to people who are just trying to live their lives. There is no reason for people of color to give white people the benefit of the doubt.

Shortly after we moved cross-country during the pandemic, Dave told me, "Would I love to explore our new neighborhood on my own? Yes, but I won't, because it wouldn't feel safe for me. I'd only do that with you." It was painful to hear how casually he said this, because he's so used to living without the freedom of space and presumption of innocence that I and so many other white people take for granted.

We both know that proximity to me makes him appear safer and less threatening to white people. Just as he is protective of me, I am extremely protective of him. I'm not sure how much my white friends in same-race relationships feel that way. When Dave and I first started dating, white people would say to me, "I think that's so great," with this tone like I was doing some act of charity, or that we represented a post-racial fantasy. We'd also frequently get approached by white people at bars and restaurants who'd say things like, "You're just a beautiful couple." While that's nice to hear, it feels like the subtext is that we're exceptional because we've chosen to see past each other's skin color, or that we're some type of novelty that makes people feel good. The utopic ease portrayed in the media of smiling interracial couples is not a reality that I'm familiar with. Not that our relationship isn't wonderful, because it is, but because it's also complex.

I don't want to solely focus on the obstacles of a cross-racial marriage. While we inevitably learn so much from our romantic partners, I didn't realize all the joy and beauty I'd come to learn about Black culture through Dave. There is so much to celebrate. We make a point to watch documentaries and TV shows, go to art exhibits, and read books that center Blackness through a Black lens together. It's a joy and privilege to be his partner.

When You Really F*ck Up

I know that as a white partner there will be times when I fail my husband and let him down. And there have absolutely been times when I have. Recently, I suggested that Dave start incorporating more skincare into his routine. My suggestions became more insistent when I saw he was resistant, until he said, point-blank: "Stop policing my Black body." Because I don't have Black skin, I don't know what's best for Black skin, he said. At first, I felt defensive, and then terrible. But I'm so grateful that he was direct with me. Our partnership shouldn't be a place where he ever feels policed, and I saw how supremacist my "I know best" point of view was.

At our Kinswomen events, Yseult often brings up the hypocrisy of white people who will fight against, for example, anti-CRT (critical race theory) parents who don't want racism taught in schools, while silencing others in a similar way in their own interactions. The incident with Dave showed me how this hypocrisy showed up in my behavior. I've worked with my city on creating oversight for our local police department, but in my own home, I was policing my husband. We need to recognize where our political ideologies contradict our personal behavior.

What other measures do I take to ensure that we have a healthy partnership, which includes my allyship? Simply asking my partner what he needs, and if he feels supported as a Black man in our relationship is a good place to start. Over the years, we've created a space where we talk about race openly, which is why we were able to discuss the skin-care issue in a productive way. Even though it was hard for me to hear, I want my partner to feel safe to express himself in a world that doesn't support the full range of emotions from men, let alone Black men.

As I said earlier, having a beginner's mindset and that of a forever student is the only way to approach being an aspiring ally, and that also applies to being a good partner. Because white supremacy is omnipresent, everything must be considered in our partnership: where we live, where I shop, what I support, where we travel, who we spend time with, and what we consume in our downtime.

Sometimes, paradoxes arise, and I have to hold space for two truths. As mentioned, we live in a place where Dave doesn't want to go exploring off the beaten path without me, but he also loves living in a beautiful coastal town and doesn't want to be denied proximity to the ocean and fresh air because he is a minority in the town's population. Often, he just wants to fly under the radar and live his life quietly, which I have to respect. (He granted me his permission to write about him in this book.) While he supported the Black Lives Matter protests in 2020, he did not want to partake in them, opting to protect himself from crowds and COVID-19. Several white friends invited me to protest with them, but I respected Dave's wish to not risk bringing COVID-19 into our home. The "right" move to make as an ally isn't always obvious, but conversation allows space for nuance. Asking and listening are underrated tools, especially in long-term relationships where a lot gets shorthanded. What's not communicated is bound to be complicated.

One of my husband's worries about being with a white woman was my white family, and what kind of potential racism he could be exposing himself to with them. That kind of worry is warranted. At first, they did not fully grasp what it meant to have a Black man join our family, and uncomfortable, even potentially dangerous situations did arise. For example, one Christmas my sister and her friends were smoking weed, and one of her friends had an anxiety attack from a bad high. Panicked, my mom called 911 and the paramedics showed up. Because the call was drug-related and we lived in a small town without its own police force in a state where marijuana wasn't legal, the state troopers showed up. "We don't want to ruin your Christmas," they said, after taking a look around, confiscating my sister's bowl, and leaving.

Afterward, my family laughed about the incident, but I was furious. When the state troopers walked into our home with Dave standing there, my mind imagined the worst. They could have taken one look at Dave and arrested him. What would the troopers have done if we had been a Black family instead of a white one? I was livid with my family members for being so flippant, and it was a point of pain and contention for months until they finally understood the privilege of being so casual with drug use and having law enforcement visit our home, and the threat that that posed to Dave. It was something that I, too, should have anticipated, bringing him to our small, mostly white town.

Being a part of a Black family has been a new experience for me, too. When we first met, I worried if Dave's family would accept me, or if they secretly wished he'd ended up with a Black woman instead. They were incredibly welcoming, and getting to know each member of his family has been a gift.

Mistakes don't just happen in romantic relationships—I've made similar mistakes in my friendship with Yseult and other friends of color. Yseult and I spend so much time together and run a platform about race, so inevitably, tensions arise, almost always race-related, since we cannot always untangle our friendship from our work. She has very high standards for me, which I appreciate. But as two strong-minded, oldest-sibling-of-three, emotional water signs, things can get heated between us. I admit, I don't always see her perspective right away, and it's that gap of time between my denial and defensiveness and then later, my understanding, that I think causes the most harm. I'm always working to close that gap.

Even in a relationship filled with love, communication, and respect, racism is likely to happen in an interracial partnership or friendship. Of course, racism happens in white-on-white relationships all the time, too, but the difference is that it may go untested or unseen because there is no visible "victim." In both cases, if our racism goes unchallenged, either by ourselves or our partners or friends, those beliefs are brought into workplaces, grocery stores, on vacation—leaked into society and then passed down to future generations.

The Complexities of Interracial Families

The famous 1967 *Loving v. Virginia* case, which declared that laws banning interracial marriages were unconstitutional and violated the Fourteenth Amendment, was only passed about fifty-five years ago. That's recent enough that our parents and grandparents were alive in a time when interracial marriage and interracial sex was illegal in certain states.

The case's defendants were Mildred Loving, a woman of color who identified as Rappahannock, African American, and Portuguese, and Richard Loving, a white man. The two met in high school and got married in DC to avoid Virginia's Act to Preserve Racial Integrity, which didn't recognize their marriage as legal. In fact, it was considered a felony. Eventually, their case made it to the Supreme Court, which ruled in favor of their marriage 9-0. And though it was signed into law, it was decades until interracial marriage was accepted in society (and we're not fully there yet). I'm so grateful that I have the freedom to love and marry whom I choose.

Every couple has major decisions about parenting to consider when thinking about having children. For us, we will have a biracial child whose experience of their race will be different from both of ours. I worry about our child feeling split between two identities, or having to explain themselves to others, or not feeling like they're Black enough or white enough. I think about raising a biracial child in a world that might want to erase, exoticize, or vilify their Blackness. I think about all the ways I could fail my child as a white woman who will never fully understand their experiences.

I know that I have a responsibility to prepare for the needs of my Black child, to learn how to tend to their hair and skin and honor and preserve their natural beauty and Blackness. To make sure my non-Black family and loved ones are equipped with the tools, language, and education to help raise a Black child. I know we will fear the adultification that Black children are subjected to by white adults who don't extend the same assumption of innocence to Black children as they do to white children. I fear the presumption of threat and the hypersexualization that white society projects onto innocent Black boys and girls. I must make sure that they see people who look like them in all the spaces they occupy as well as in the education and media that they're exposed to.

These are questions that I and all white parents and adults should be asking ourselves: whether we are participating in creating a harmful culture for children of color with our own biases and assumptions about them. For example, we must stop fetishizing mixed children. The frequency that I hear "mixed babies are the *cutest*" is absurd. Black, Brown, or Asian children are not more beautiful when mixed with whiteness. In 2020, I attended a Zoom event with Layla F. Saad where she talked about the "pet to threat" tipping point for kids of color. The reality is that the years between the "cute" fetishization age and the "call the cops" age is tragically short.

Interracial families require special care and consideration. We see so many examples in the media of white parents adopting Black or Asian children. Though often the narrative has been that the white parents are saintly heroes whose kids are so lucky to have been "rescued" by them, the experience of a transracial adoptee can be traumatic, their identity having been erased or overlooked by white parents who thought it was best to not see their color.

In 2020, a white YouTube couple, Myka and James Stauffer, parents to several white children and an autistic toddler adopted from China, "unadopted" their Chinese son after he displayed behavioral issues.[27] Followers noticed that the child had stopped appearing in posts, and the couple tearfully admitted to giving him to another family. The backlash was intense. It seemed as if the decision to adopt him in the first place—which was extensively chronicled on their YouTube channel—was based on strengthening their own personal brand instead of doing what was best for the child. While this example of an interracial family may seem extreme, it illustrates how white parents often do not know or cannot provide what a transracial adoptee needs, and they can be harmful to the child, despite the selfless, heroic narrative of transracial adoption.

Cross-Racial Dialogues in Media & Culture

As we mentioned in chapter two, trust is the most important element of a cross-racial friendship or relationship, and it's built in part by listening to and validating one another's experiences. It's not okay for us to want a diverse group of friends but not want to hear about why their experiences are different from ours. After years of mostly avoiding politics, race, and social justice issues, mainstream white pop culture has just begun to stumble through these dialogues on a public platform.

As a longtime watcher of the *Real Housewives* franchise on Bravo, I've felt uncomfortable, angry, and hopeful watching the

---

27 https://www.thecut.com/2020/08/youtube-myka-james-stauffer-huxley-adoption.html.

women across various cities broach conversations on race in recent seasons. There's been both bigotry and moments of beautiful truth. As the theater that is reality TV does best, the women's messy internal dialogues are surfaced and debated with their fellow castmates while the world watches. A white viewer sitting on the couch in Tennessee may have the exact same thoughts as a conservative white cast member, but seeing it verbalized and then reacted to by a Black woman is a chain of events that may not ever happen in that viewer's real life. My husband, a part-time viewer, has punched the air in catharsis after seeing Black cast members speak their truths openly.

In 2021, we saw similar breakdowns and breakthroughs happen on *The Talk*, in the podcast series *Test Kitchen*, and in Meghan Markle and Prince Harry's interview with Oprah about the racism Meghan and her child faced from the Royal Family. It is fascinating to witness cross-racial discourse between friends and colleagues (and royals) happen on large platforms. For as long as it took us to get here, and as awkward as these conversations are, we can learn from them; they likely reflect what's happening in friend groups, families, and workplaces across the country. When we hear people of color share their truths on a national platform—or anywhere—we should listen and think about how those same dynamics are happening in our own lives.

Everything Hannah mentions resonates with me, and I'd add that the way these things play out on-screen is so predictable and boring. Reality TV in particular focuses on raw emotions and outbursts, but it doesn't take time to ask why people act the way they do. (I mean mainly for BIPOC present in these spaces.) I know these scenarios and dramas aren't meant to portray real life. The issues presented are real, but in reality, people's interactions are often more subtle.

Socially, we aren't at a place where these subjects can be

trivialized the way they are on TV and other major platforms without people getting angry and hurt. I know nobody watches the *Housewives* for education or real-life insight, but when conversations about race aren't had elsewhere, it adds to how dehumanized BIPOC are and how these real-life situations—that have real consequences and trauma—become entertainment. It exhausts me.

I may be an idealist and dreamer, but I think if not in America, where else are these issues tackled in such a direct way? In many ways the US has a lot more work to do, but it's also a place where some of the most change has happened the fastest compared to other colonial powers in the world. For example, South Africa only abolished apartheid in 1994, and France is still collecting a decolonization tax on "ex"-colonies. England is holding on to the countries where the monarch of England is head of state—fifteen to be exact, including Jamaica, St. Lucia, St. Kitts and Nevis, Grenada, and Papua New Guinea. Most of the countries in the Commonwealth realm are made up of people of color. My perception of the US may come off as harsh, but really, it's because I have higher hopes for this country. I admire and look up to the BIPOC advocates who are fighting to make lasting changes here.

I love seeing how the noise made in the streets of America has a ripple effect on the rest of the world. I find the copycat effect productive because white supremacy is everywhere, but it also manifests and plays out differently if you're in New York compared to a city like Brussels, where protests sometimes feel like a miss when they use the same American slogan but ignore issues that are specific to their own cities. It's a nuanced conversation because the people and issues at play aren't the same, but I still love it because we have to start somewhere. I don't think change happens fast enough, but I've witnessed how our society can be forced to listen and sometimes, make swift changes.

YSEULT P. MUKANTABANA & HANNAH SUMMERHILL

★ ★ ★

As white people who participate in interracial relationships or friendships, we cannot be naive to the power dynamics that exist in our relationships and in our wider culture. We are never starting with a clean slate and cannot ignore the history of harm between us. If we want to have more or healthier relationships with those outside of our own race, we must acknowledge that bringing our whiteness to the relationship is not a neutral thing, and be willing to listen, without trying to erase or avoid what's painful for us to hear. The complexities should be something we get curious about, welcome, and respect, instead of trying to simplify them into something more palatable. The responsibility is on us as white people to do more intellectual and emotional work so that we stop inflicting suffering on people of color, and so that we may *all* thrive.

EIGHT

Social Justice on Social Media

A Performative Allyship Performance Space

Performative allyship seems to flourish on social media; it's where the phenomenon best comes to life. White people can easily "copy/paste" how much they care by sharing quickly made, easy-to-understand slides about matters that shouldn't and can't be summed up in a few digital graphics. This applies to issues that aren't just about race, but all the heated topics that people feel the need to add their own pinch of opinions—often *uninformed*—to the messy soup of digital media.

Social media is an amazing place to read neatly packaged quotes and stories that provide just enough content for dinner party conversation before a big election or after a horrific act of violence, so that the "liberal and non-racist" badge feels legit. It's a lazy way to absorb information and reinforces the idea that individual accountability doesn't have to exist beyond the screen.

★ ★ ★

It's also very possible to cause actual harm online, even when we intend to be an ally. In the summer of 2020, many white people reposted the murder of George Floyd to their Instagram or Facebook feeds, thinking that it would help motivate others into action, or to show their outrage. However, there was a call from the Black community for white people to stop posting images and videos of Black people dying. Yes, it was our responsibility as white people to watch it, but not ours to share it, and by doing so, we were potentially adding to the trauma of people of color who'd see it while scrolling.

I truly cannot imagine what the uproar from white people would have been if it was Black people posting white people being murdered. Although those who shared the video thought they were doing the virtuous thing, to me, it showed how limited our view and value of Black life was by the way we so casually disseminated images of Black death. In allyship, our actions should be carefully considered, and we need to listen to feedback from the communities most affected and center their experiences over our own.

It's important to remember that our seemingly insignificant opinions online can create a snowball effect of bad information that can make people uncomfortable and sometimes even unsafe. An example that comes to mind is the conflict between Israel and Palestine.

I cannot claim to be an expert, and I'm even less comfortable going online to tell people what needs to be done to fix this particular social and political situation. What I do realize is that the misinformation and often antisemitic rhetoric posted online makes Jewish people feel unsafe, and for the Jewish communities that are visible, they experience real life-threatening attacks, because people think hurting someone will "fix" the problem.

I've spent a lot of time trying to dissect the phenomenon of performative allyship. If you want to witness it, take a tour through the cyberspace savanna of Instagram's anti-racist mirages and stop by the comments section. That's where white allyship performance is at an all-time high. Everyone seems to care about having a perfect answer to topics that they don't know anything about, and honestly, I don't expect white people to have those answers.

I see this happening a lot in the comments section of Rachel Cargle's posts. She's an amazing speaker, advocate, and educator who posts about complex topics. When I read her posts, even as a Black woman, I need time to digest everything she says. Her posts are so vulnerable and stir up a lot of emotions, so I try to process my feelings first before responding. I feel her posts deserve space to exist without me jumping in with my own opinions. Her words make me feel seen and understood, and yet it feels weird to comment and make it about myself. I want to make sure that I can take time to digest and humanize her words. While I feel like I need to take a second to meditate on her posts, I've noticed a lot of white commenters not taking the same thought or care with their responses. It doesn't seem like they're interested in engaging with the subject, but instead catering to their own sense of entitlement and performative allyship.

In Rachel's comments section, there are some wild things happening under the posts about race. First, you have the fragile white type, who are supposedly in shock over Cargle's post and make it about themselves. Their guilt cannot be contained, and they'll write something that boils down to "All Lives Matter" or "We aren't ALL like this." You also have the "OMG WE ARE THE WORST" type of white person, who insists on how horrible they are, and you're basically witnessing social media flagellation. This type of person makes me feel the most uncomfortable. It doesn't feel genuine at all. The point of the post isn't to provoke self-inflicted and unnecessary insults. It would be much more productive for commenters to consider how this information is offering a new perspective, and to be honest and open about how they have personally participated in that particular issue.

But my favorite kind of commenter is the one that jumps in to chime in on the callout of a white person's behavior without even taking time to think that just *maybe* they are guilty of that behavior, too. They don't take time to reflect and think about their own impact; instead, they point fingers at other white people and become "teachers." At best, those are the people who have read five anti-racist books, went to a workshop about social justice, and might even date or are married to a BIPOC. At worst, it's the person that never says anything when they see something out of fear of making people uncomfortable and being rejected by their group of friends, but suddenly now that someone else points out problematic behavior and it feels "right" to "speak up" do they. They jump to point fingers at others instead of taking a beat and calling themselves out for saying nothing and owning up to their silence.

They are maybe the most harmful ones. They've given themselves a badge of allyship, you can't tell them anything, and they think they've done all the work necessary. If there was a diploma to hand out for being an ally, they are convinced they'd get a PhD.

The Harmful Hierarchy of Advocacy on Social Media

Social media also has an "unspoken hierarchy"—I've noticed that people have decided who is and isn't worth fighting for online. For example, when there are Brown and Black people experiencing racism, I tend to see people posting and sharing their support (though this doesn't mean it's always genuine). But when the Jewish community is being attacked, then there's no solidarity—I don't see non-Jewish people post nearly as much as they do for the Black and Brown community. I've also observed that the Asian community doesn't have as many "allies" supporting them on social media.

It's like white people have a conscious or subconscious mechanism that tells them who to stand up for. I can't accept that, because the root of racism against Black, Indigenous, Brown people is the same as the hate and violence propagated against Asian and Jewish people. People who want to be anti-racists need to apply the same energy defending all minority and marginalized groups, and I would even say that people within minorities need to stand with each other whenever some act of hate happens, no matter who it's directed toward. The root disease is the same—white supremacy. It's important for people to remember that white supremacy harms both, the visible minorities and invisible, too.

It's perhaps because Jewishness is less visible than other identities, but I've noticed that advocacy against antisemitism exists differently on social media than other forms of advocacy. It's either completely left out from conversations, or only talked about in Jewish spaces by Jewish people themselves. There are not many cross-advocacy conversations that happen. It exists, but it feels rare, which is a problem. It bears repeating that all kinds of discrimination—including antisemitism—stem from the same root of ideology and hate. Leaving antisemitism out of the discussion is like trying to prevent your basement from flooding while ignoring a hole in the ceiling. There's no reality in this world where as a Black woman I'd consider myself free and safe if Jewish people were left out of the conversation of advocacy. Because all of these issues are interconnected, we must address them in collaboration with each group and community.

Activism's Short Attention Span

Social media can build people up, make them rich and famous, and it can tear them down, "canceling" them, all within a day.

It's been called a blessing, a curse, a tool, a nuisance. It's noisy. It brings people together and it tears them apart. Not a place for nuance, it creates binaries with contextless pull quotes by people who aim to out-mic-drop one another. It inspires movements, then backlash to those movements, and then backlash to the backlash. It makes you laugh and feel inspired, and then makes you feel like absolute shit. It's as wonderful and horrible as the humans who create and contribute to it. I hate it. I love it.

We spend a lot of our time on social media, and it's increasingly a place where millennials and Gen Zers get their news and express their political and social views, myself included. For aspiring allies, it may feel like "activism" online translates as actual activism, but rarely is that the case. Social media can be a tool for discovery and education, but I believe that real allyship happens off the apps.

Racial justice became a mainstream conversation for white people on social media after George Floyd's murder, in May 2020. Whether it was because the pandemic had us glued to our phones, the fact that it was four hundred years overdue, or both, the treatment of Black lives in America could no longer be ignored.

One ubiquitous response to the racial reckoning was the posting of a black square to our Instagram pages, with the caption #blackouttuesday, in early June 2020. This gesture, it seemed, was not so much in solidarity with Black lives, but in solidarity with the other accounts that posted a black square. Individuals who had never spoken about racial justice online, or brands who'd never had a Black model grace their feeds weren't concerned about violence to Black bodies, but rather, *appearing* like they weren't concerned.

The black square devolved from the hashtag #TheShowMustBePaused, started by Jamila Thomas and Brianna Agyemang, two Black women in the music industry, who wrote: "Our mission is to hold the industry at large, including major corporations + their partners who benefit from the effort, struggles and successes of Black people accountable."[28] The "pause" then became the black square, often hashtagged with #blacklivesmatter, which buried any relevant information on the movement under millions of black squares.

During that heated time, almost every single brand and company used social media as a space to make knee-jerk commitments of donating money to BIPOC organizations and investing in their company's anti-racism education. They were "listening to learning." Very few companies were clear about why it had taken them that long to start listening and learning. I can only imagine the dissonance felt by former or current employees of color at all of these companies, whose experiences most likely did not match up with the equitable values being espoused by their workplace on social media.

As the racial reckoning gained steam on the streets and online, white people scrambled to showcase our goodness. Several white celebrities and influencers participated in a "ShareTheMicNow" initiative, where Black educators or influencers took over the accounts of white celebs and influencers for the day. Just a day. Now that we're a few years past this "state of emergency," it's clear that the black squares and the passed mics were as significant and fleeting as a made-up Instagram holiday.

Similar to the way #metoo spread across social media in the wake of learning about Harvey Weinstein's longtime abuse and we tried to immediately rectify a culture of deeply normalized misogyny and sexual trauma, the murders of George Floyd, Ahmaud Arbery, and Breonna Taylor prompted white panic, despair, awakening, and a pressure to act immediately.

There was some progress, and there were some casualties. Celebrities, influencers, and brands had their problematic racial histories aired across social media, causing firings, loss of sponsorship deals, and (maybe only temporarily) cratered careers.

---

28   https://www.vulture.com/2020/06/blackout-tuesday-guide.html.

White people were finally paying attention and maybe even recognizing the impact of our apathy and inaction. But for how long would we care?

The enthusiasm was ephemeral. White people who live streamed their participation in the Black Lives Matter protests in the summer of 2020 had moved on by the fall. Reports have shown that only a fraction of the millions of dollars that were promised to Black organizations was made good on. Many retailers and companies signed The 15 Percent Pledge started by Aurora James, founder of the brand Brother Vellies, vowing to commit a minimum of 15 percent of their shelf space to Black-owned businesses.[29] Brands like Crate & Barrel, *Vogue*, Sephora, Rent the Runway, and Gap have signed the pledge. It is now on those companies to transparently show their progress in meeting those goals with the public, and it's on the public to hold them to their promises.

While I know that outrage isn't necessarily sustainable, our attention spans are tragically short when it comes to anti-racism. As white people, we shouldn't only be motivated by social pressure or by seeing trauma in the news. We each have a personal responsibility to continue the conversation, educate ourselves, and to take anti-racist action. So why aren't we?

These are questions we should ask ourselves when it comes to our relationship with social justice and social media: Am I worried that posting about social justice is "off-brand" and will annoy people? Do I only have incentive to care and share about racial issues when everyone else is doing the same? What is really stopping me from speaking up?

A lot of white silence comes from fear of saying or posting the wrong thing, and then being subject to public feedback or even our biggest fear as white people: cancellation. *Cancellation* has become a catchall phrase for accountability, public shame, being let go from a job, and in some cases, actual, justified can-

---

29   https://www.15percentpledge.org.

cellation. I know that I, along with many, harbor a fear of cancellation as the "worst" thing that could happen to us: that our racism, past or present, will be exposed. But that's not an excuse to be silent.

If racist tweets from 2012 surface, for example, we must own up to them, make apologies, and share what we're doing to mitigate the harm caused. The threat of being "canceled" scares us into inaction, when really, it's okay—and human—to make mistakes, learn from them, and take accountability. If we're going to share something as intimate as pictures of our newborn babies, why can't we also share our values about issues that affect humans, or be vulnerable enough to admit when we've done wrong?

In our work, Yseult and I tell our clients and students to make their values clear, whether it's on social media or their website, and to be consistent with it. One fashion brand we worked with wrote a thorough anti-racism mission statement that appeared proudly on their site for a few months, only to be taken down by the end of 2020. Maybe they had a hard time maintaining those promises, or maybe they thought it might alienate customers after the uproar died down. If you as a brand or individual didn't come through on your statements and promises, you only added to the noise. Let's normalize sharing the work that we're doing and how we're upholding the promises that we made. Transparency and accountability should be the bare minimum.

Companies should not just be clear about their values and invest in anti-racism work because they fear bad PR, financial ruin, or getting canceled. Post–June 2020, popular but problematic shows like *Cops* and *Live PD* were taken off the air, and episodes of *30 Rock*, *It's Always Sunny in Philadelphia*, *Scrubs*, *Community*, and *Golden Girls* were removed from streaming services for portraying blackface.[30] But rarely are we erasing or taking away the power of those who have been "canceled." The fame

---

30   https://www.thewrap.com/movies-tv-shows-canceled-blacklives-matter-cops-gone-with-the-wind/.

and followers usually remain, so the social currency doesn't budge. Sometimes there are financial repercussions, like sponsorship opportunities lost, but "cancel culture" has demanded accountability from only a few.

However, sometimes our reactionary damage control too swiftly puts issues and people into good/bad or right/wrong categories, and we miss opportunities to discuss the nuances that race conversations require. Social media reinforces the need for quick and easy answers, compressing complex conversations into 2D squares as we try to prove that we're less racist than the white person next to us, or find tidy solutions to deeply entangled social issues.

It's frustrating to witness how ephemeral our reaction to injustice is—the interest, fight, sharing, and outrage—until another video or article comes out to "revive" the topic. It seems like white people believe that if something is not in front of them, then things got better. Take, for instance, when COVID-19 was at its all-time high in New York. Each evening at a designated time, people would gather around windows and sidewalks and clap to honor the healthcare workers on the frontlines. The second the media wasn't sharing alarming news and photos about the pandemic, people stopped honoring their "heroes." Life returned to some kind of normal and people moved on. Healthcare workers' pay didn't suddenly increase from the music made by all our pan banging and hand clapping.

We see the same short attention span when it comes to minorities dying at the hands of white supremacy in our streets. It's hard for me to understand why people can't understand the urgency until there's a Black body laid in front of us. We need a disturbing video to believe racial violence happens, and even then, it's brushed off as just another name added to countless other Black people killed for no other reason but the color of their skin. "My skin can get me killed" is a sentence that I know is true, but it's still hard for my mind to grasp. The cry from communities, the marches, and the protests aren't enough when minorities are still losing their lives. My humanity is worth more than a social media life cycle.

There are positive ways, however, that social media can be used. Since social media caters images and posts to us based on what we like and who we follow, we can customize the kind of content we're regularly exposed to. Personally, I've found a whole range of people and posts that bring solace to me, especially as a Black woman. I love that my feed feeds me content that pushes me to learn. I can find other Black people sharing narratives that humanize me and that help recharge my batteries and ground me in my already existing values. I've especially loved being able to find communities that I couldn't find as easily otherwise, as I am Jewish and Black. I have been able to find people online that experience this same intersection that feels so niche, and when I do, it's like a little piece of me is filled in.

I'll be the first to say that it's not easy to find the information and narratives that will help you on your journey to relearning. It's there, but it takes longer and more intentional action to locate. This can be challenging because social media as a whole sells itself as accessible and easy, which doesn't lend itself well to people taking extra steps. We have access to so many narratives through a variety of mediums; we can expand our realities and we have no excuse not to.

I realize this positive take on social media may come across as childlike or naive, but my enthusiasm is fueled by my Rwandan roots and how we have moved and grown from our history. If Rwanda can rise and thrive as a people and nation the way we have and continue to in only twenty-eight years, I know anything is possible. I am also very conscious that the only way real change and shift in perspective is possible is when people can take accountability, responsibility, and are willing to do the necessary work out of love. Faith alone doesn't do it.

White People's Success for Black People's Work

In 2020, some social media accounts capitalized on the anxiety of white people who were realizing how little we knew. One Instagram account, called @soyouwanttotalkabout, sprang up in February of that year as a daily explainer on social justice issues in slideshow format, in an effort to promote Bernie Sanders in the 2020 primaries. The account's popularity grew during the racial uprising in 2020, and many followers assumed it was run by or associated with Ijeoma Oluo, a Black woman whose bestselling 2018 book *So You Want to Talk About Race* has a very similar title.

In reality, the account was run by Jessica Natale, a twenty-something white woman whose identity seemed intentionally ambiguous, and not Ijeoma Oluo, as many assumed. Wondering who was behind the account, Oluo said on her Instagram stories that she messaged the account to ask who was running it, and that her question went unanswered. After that, Oluo said that she assumed the account was run by a white person, "otherwise they wouldn't ignore the question." Oluo blocked the account, and eventually the account included a disclaimer in their bio that they were not associated with Oluo.

But the controversy gained steam when Natale got a book deal based on the success of @soyouwanttotalkabout, which had grown to almost three million followers in 2021. The backlash was swift, and accountability was demanded. Natale changed the name of her account to @so.informed, vowed to be clearer about who her collaborators were, announced that the book deal was on pause, and issued a public and private apology to Ijeoma Oluo. On her Instagram stories in 2021, Oluo called the account "duplicitous, shady, and harmful" for capitalizing off the work of a Black woman.

The controversy brought up my own feelings about being a white woman cowriting a book about race and bridging the gaps. I do not claim to be an educator, but instead, share my thoughts on white impact and white responsibility, including my own. I could name all the differences between myself and Natale—that I'm writing this book with Yseult and wouldn't and couldn't do it alone, that there is space and a need for our voices to be heard together, that I wouldn't have capitalized on and dishonored Ms. Oluo's work and requests—but of course, I fear the same kind of criticism.

According to Oluo, Natale was cognizant of what she was doing and the impact it was having on Oluo. She capitalized off Oluo's work and success, which is wrong. But I don't place all the blame on Natale for her millions of followers, or for her book deal. The responsibility is also on white followers to know where we're getting our information from. No lazy follows! And her publisher should have considered that it would be problematic for a white women to position herself as an expert on social justice issues before offering her a book deal. We need to do our due diligence with our teachers and educators.

We've seen so many public Instagram apologies from white women that they've practically become their own genre (Audrey Gelman, Alison Roman, Ellie Kemper). Though these apologies are for the people of color harmed, and not for white people, inevitably, white followers will accept the apology in the comments section anyway, with sentiments like, "Thank you, you are so brave." There's this impulse for us as white people to applaud another white person for a public apology, when it's not for us.

In her Instagram stories, Ijeoma Oluo shared why she thought that the work of @soyouwanttotalkabout was harmful. "I am not interested in the 'meme-ification' of anti-racist and social justice work." That really struck me, because it's tempting to feel like learning from these digestible slides or memes is enough on its own, instead of taking what we're learning offline.

While these formats can help build awareness and offer top-line info and context, how can the lessons really be applied if the format of Instagram pushes us to…instantly go to the next 'gram? Depending on your algorithm, you could go from reparations to 2000s fashion in less than a second (or maybe that's just my feed). For me, I can only really learn and integrate anti-racism work when I read, watch documentaries, or interact with humans. Working against our internalized white supremacy requires real time spent, and we owe the work the respect of our undivided attention so that we may integrate it, share it, and be it.

On our own *Kinswomen* account, I struggle with this. We want to bring people in and nurture a space to learn, but the realities of the platform foster inattentiveness, immediacy, and quick fixes. All of that is the antithesis of anti-racism work. I'm turned off by the idea of feeding the content beast, but I also know that our work has value and should be shared. I don't have the answers and it feels like a balance we're constantly trying to find. I *do* learn a lot from following social justice educators on social media, but I also know that it's my responsibility not to stop there when I put my phone down.

The Most Important Work Happens Offline

Most of us might admit that our Internet presence doesn't accurately reflect our offline lives. Reposting or following social justice accounts does not make us allies if our own lives don't involve activism. I find it frustrating when aspiring allies repost about anti-racism or social justice without adding in their own learnings, reflections, or calls-to-action, and instead let other people's words speak for them, appropriating the work, effort, and bravery that it took that educator to post for themselves. This kind of low-commitment effort has been referred to as "slacktivism."

When I'm posting about allyship or anti-racism, I'm always checking my motives, and asking myself: Who is this for? Is this to keep me accountable? Am I virtue signaling? Is this actually helpful in advancing the cause? Will this motivate others? Is it in line with my values? In our offline allyship, too, we must ask ourselves if we're doing it for online accolades. I believe our lives spent away from the screen are sacred and shouldn't be lived through the lens of how they will be received on the Internet. We should be motivated enough in our own allyship to take action even when no one else knows that we did.

We must also be aware of the white lens of our own social channels, which are highly influenced to reinforce our past behavior by using algorithms to serve us more of the same. One of the easiest ways to decenter your white lens is to find accounts online that *don't* center whiteness and are run by BIPOC creators. The algorithms will present you with more of whatever you interact with most, so notice what you're being funneled, and it'll be a snapshot of your lens. I see a clear difference between my personal Instagram Discover page and *Kinswomen*'s. Because both Yseult and I share the *Kinswomen* account, the Discover page is more of a mesh of our two interests. By comparison, my own Discover page serves me lots of whiteness—more of what I engage with and what the algorithm thinks that I'll like. I have to be intentional about decentering whiteness from my feed so that it's not all that I'll see.

Because they're created by humans, I believe Instagram's algorithms are just as biased as we are. Algorithms don't exist out of thin air. Our *Kinswomen* account has been deprioritized in the algorithm for using words like *racism* and *white supremacy*, and so many Black creators have been shadow-banned, where it's believed that Instagram is hiding their work from being seen. In a supposed effort to censor hate speech, they've penalized those who are fighting against it. Whether that's intentional or not, we may never know.

There is a bright side to social media, of course, and I don't want to be dismissive of the incredible galvanizing, organizing, and fundraising that has been done on platforms like Instagram. Rachel Cargle, the Black writer and lecturer that Yseult mentioned earlier in this chapter, raised over $250,000 from her social media followers for her nonprofit, the Loveland Foundation, which provides therapy to Black women and girls nationally.[31] That's just one example of the awareness and money that has been raised to support incredible causes and individuals.

During the Black Lives Matter protests of 2020, social media acted as a global corkboard to bring awareness to and strengthen movements and marches. We've personally discovered so many incredible educators and people on Instagram that have become podcast guests, students, and friends. Social media can have a powerful and positive impact on how we show up in our lives offline as allies, but it's the offline activism that should be prioritized above the online performance.

---

31   https://thelovelandfoundation.org/about/.

NINE

Blackfishing, Digital Blackface, and Cultural Appropriation

I don't think we spend enough time considering how racism and its different facets adapt and morph, and how the digital space is a new frontier for it to exist in. Racism is in everything and it's everywhere. It's not just a sentiment; it's a settled system put in place to maintain and empower white supremacy. Racism feels like a big monster when I explain it that way, but the way I experience the world, racism manifests in so many ways. The digital space is a modern medium of expression and communication, but we're dealing with the same people and power dynamics of white supremacy.

For example, racism in the digital world is obvious with gifs. As a Black woman, I don't get to express myself online at the same level as white people because the range of gif emotions is never as broad and available for BIPOC. When I look up the word *shy* in the gif library, images of white men, women, or adorable animals are the first to appear. I have to resort to using kittens or puppies when I want to send a "shy" gif, because shyness is something that's predominantly attributed to white people or cute animals. And it's true in real life, too, isn't it? Try imagining a shy little girl. I know people aren't picturing a Black little girl. If you type "punk rock person" into the gif library, you'll see a white girl or boy with spiked-up hair and a guitar. In real life, if you play the game with white friends to see what they imagine when you refer to certain emotions or feelings, they will for sure imagine a white person without considering that it could be also a person of color.

I remember when I first discovered *Awkward Black Girl*, a comedic web series created and produced by Issa Rae. She's now a very successful and well-known actress and producer, but in 2011, I discovered her on YouTube. I felt seen in her work because I never thought I could relate to such characteristics. Black girls aren't seen as awkward or shy, but rather the sidekick that "empowers" or "holds down" their white main character. Asian characters also hold that special sidekick role a lot. Issa Rae made me feel seen and like I could just be myself in all ways. It's funny how that has stuck with me for so long, and I think it's because of how rare it was and still is to see Black characters break through stereotypes and societal norms.

I'm still actively working to live in my whole truth and not one that is digestible to people. I read somewhere in the wise book of Instagram not to make myself small to be digestible, but rather "let people choke." This is from a place of love. The digital realm often reflects all they ways white supremacy intends to keep Black people one-dimensional.

Blackfishing Isn't Flattery

Copycatting is also a staple of white supremacy: "discovering" something someone has been doing for centuries and passing it as your own is a classic move. It's the oppressor and conqueror mindset that is seen in everything and everywhere— music, art, science, and so on. Now we have words that define these phenomena, which is a relief, and can better articulate everything we have collectively experienced.

I'm reminded of a conversation I had with my little niece, Yura. She's thirteen years old, and a bright, spitting image of her mother, my dear cousin Katia. I hadn't seen her in a while and couldn't get over how cute she was. We were at a French restaurant somewhere in Kigali. My mother booked the spot for my uncle's birthday. We all ordered from a very "French menu," and as I'm vegetarian I didn't have much choice. Yura decided she would have spaghetti Bolognese, pasta with ground meatballs in tomato sauce. I got some fries and steamed veggies. Yura was just about to take her first dive into her pasta when she then looked up and said, "Ata, we're in a French restaurant, right?" I responded affirmatively and she proceeded to say, "Well, this pasta isn't really French, it's an Italian dish, and the French fries are Belgian, so why is this restaurant saying it's French if we are eating things that aren't French?" I laughed and whispered that we live in a colonized world where people take things and claim it as their own. She made an *"oh"* sound and I instantly felt like I had officially become "that type of aunt."

Jokes aside, appropriation causes real harm, and it erases and minimizes cultures that have been told that they aren't normal, beautiful, or worthy of contribution to humanity, which is just a gross lie. We're in a time where, more than ever, we have amazing access to others' lives and cultures, so it's normal that we take a little from each other. But my real issue with appropriation is when it harms and oppresses BIPOC while white people benefit from it. It isn't right.

As white people, we love taking what we want from other cultures and ditching the rest. We are a society obsessed with consumption—we try it and then we trash it. While traditional blackface may be less prevalent, we've found other, newer ways to be culture vultures that we'll likely regret in just a few years.

One way that this theft has manifested in the social media age is through *Blackfishing*, a term accredited to journalist Wanna Thompson.[32] Blackfishing is when non–Black people (usually women) appropriate features, makeup, and hairstyles that are intrinsic to Black culture, like fuller lips, darker skin, cornrows, and curves in an effort to exoticize ourselves. Thompson has said, "White women want access to Blackness but don't want the suffering that comes along with it."[33]

Some say that the greatest form of flattery is imitation. When it comes to something like Blackfishing, I don't find it flattering, but rather, insulting. It's problematic especially in relation to the physical features that define my Blackness that I was often teased about. I grew up around boys when I was a child, and men when I got older, who would fetishize and sexualize things like my lips. I felt for the longest time like they weren't beautiful, and I wished that I could have flat ones like my white friends and other people around me. The attention on my lips was never positive; rather, I felt like I had to make them small and erase them.

Fast-forward to today and in more recent years, people, mainly thin-lipped individuals that happen to be predominantly white, are getting lip injections. I think of my younger self. If only I could go back and tell her that others would end up being envious of what they made fun of me for. It's a weird dynamic then to see that something that was ridiculed on me is now desired by the same people. I remember being complimented by white people for my "small features" like it was something that was exceptional to see on us Black people.

32 http://www.wannasworld.com/.

33 https://www.papermag.com/white-women-blackfishing-instagram-2619714094.html.

Meanwhile, I grew up seeing so many white people with big noses, for example. Those noses weren't put under scrutiny or considered undesirable except when they were on Jewish people, of course, because they were used for caricatures to vilify them in the propaganda before and during WWII. There's a movement of empowerment to reclaim beauty standards that have been whitewashed. I always knew that the kids and adults who commented on my body were really commenting on themselves.

Another feature that has shifted in being desirable is the butt. Growing up I remember a specific moment when I realized that I didn't have to look like the mannequins I saw on display in stores. Naturally, women from where I am from are shaped like beautiful guitars. They are beautiful and carry themselves with grace. They sway into the room as if someone were snapping a picture for every movement. This is a subjective opinion, but I am not exaggerating when I say that in Rwanda we have among the most beautiful women of the continent, if not the world. Obviously, all Black women are the most beautiful beings in this world! That has been something I was blessed to realize and internalize very young.

I'll never forget the special moment I shared with yet another aunt of mine. Marie-Jean is one of my favorite aunts, and just like all my aunts, she's so beautiful. I remember loving when she and my mother would hang out. We would all pack up and head to the park with my little cousin Helena, who was the youngest girl in the family, and everyone, me included, treated her like a little princess. Except maybe my brother Ricky, who would wrestle her because that's how she wanted to play with him, until someone got hurt and she would run to me or my mother. We were close and I saw my aunt MJ as one of the most beautiful women ever.

One day we went to the city center to shop together. I remember loving an outfit displayed in a store's window. I turned to MJ and said so. She quickly replied, "Let's go try it on." I refused and explained to her that I didn't think I could wear it because I didn't have the right body. I'm an '80s baby so I never got to see people with different shades and shapes on display. The standard was the no-hips-no-butt white-looking mannequins that I could never relate to.

She very casually said, "Yseult, you don't need to look like them to wear that." That sentence stuck with me, and it made so much sense, but I had to hear it externally. I know that body issues and body representation aren't exclusive to Black women. Women in general are judged and forced by our culture to look a certain way. It's just that when you experience subliminal or straight-up racism about your body, all those little things add up. I'm so thankful that growing up I had women and people around me that helped make me comfortable with my body.

I know I share the same stories with other BIPOC. If beauty standards changed in a way that we all benefited from them, I wouldn't even care. I get mad when a famous white woman with a big rear is considered sexy and appealing, but when we look at Black women in the spotlight, we are told to hide our body and minimize it because it's seen as "vulgar, ghetto." We need to remember that before Kim K. there were artists like Foxy Brown and Lil' Kim who embraced and proudly showcased their natural assets in the public eye. When it comes to Blackfishing, I wish people would take time to understand and humanize the frustration and anger of BIPOC. It's not like we're haters not wanting others to live their best lives—it's just that there's a double beauty standard that we are tired of. It's harmful and traumatizing when you can't be comfortable in your skin.

Digital Blackface

I'm a good texter…when I don't forget to reply! I love to use gifs, as I think it gives life to a written conversation and also helps with misunderstandings because texting can come off as dry. My closest friends know that my gif game is strong. As a Black woman though, I realize that of course, among everything else, gifs are put together from a whitewashed point of view and algorithm. My selection compared to white people is minimal, and as earlier mentioned, I have to opt for animals or animation to express things like shyness, awkwardness, silliness, and other emotions too often illustrated by and from a white person's view.

Just to help visualize what I mean, try using an app like GIF to type one of the emotions that I named and see what images come up. Most of the images are of white characters, real or animated; you won't or rarely will see a BIPOC gif. If anything could be a good indicator of the lack of representation it would be this app. I personally feel weird using white characters to express myself in imagery—it doesn't sit well with me. I could type in the name of the actresses, singers, or specific characters that I know I have seen before as a workaround, but it's exhausting. If I don't see myself in gifs, the next best thing is to use animated characters, or cute animals so that I don't feel weird.

On the other hand, if I want to express feelings and attitudes that are "characteristic" to Black people, then I have plenty of choices. If I want to show sassiness, attitude, pettiness, anger, and the like, I will have a load of Black characters to choose from. I am sure that you are starting to see the weirdness of it all. Gifs can be a good marker of how we are evolving, because technically, they're a collection of stills from shows, movies, and all types of entertainment. We don't usually see roles in media where Black people are shy, awkward, or weird, so there are fewer gifs for those emotions. We aren't thought of in our full humanity.

The wild part and disturbing side to this is that white people now have a new way to express blackface. It's not as disgusting as the classic painted-Black face, but digital blackface is when a white person uses the voice or image of Black people for their content in the form of gifs and memes. These are often pulled from shows where BIPOC are all too often represented in a way that fits the whitewashed idea of who we are, and feels like a mockery of real Black people. So, you have Amber who feels comfortable using a NeNe Leakes gif to express how she feels, not because she's shy, but rather to mimic Blackness. It's really cringe. My point of view may seem limiting and annoying, but I don't care. We are still mimicking caricatures that are meant to amuse the white masses and dehumanize us in the process. It may feel small, but small things add up to big things. I think it's important to spend time naming and explaining these social phenomena.

Over time racism has morphed and adapted to our current culture, from live theater to books, TV, and now the Internet and metaverse. Racism transpires in all of these spaces. I want people to understand this and learn to see it. Even if it looks like a cute trend, it's important we avoid these things. The Black body continues to be dehumanized and mocked, which then makes it possible to feel desensitized when Black bodies are harmed. Children are seen as adults before they have had time to live their youth; Black women are looked over; and Black men are feared and posed as threatening people that need to be detained. These things creep up into our minds and imaginations and shape us to see the world a specific way. I hope reading this section can help you to see digital blackface for what it is and avoid feeding into it.

Try It & Trash It

As Yseult mentioned, little acts of appropriation accumulate in having a larger cultural impact and causing actual harm. If you're white, you might cringe thinking back on the cornrows you got on vacation in Jamaica in middle school, or the cheongsam dress you wore to junior year homecoming. At the time, these choices most likely seemed benign. Cultural appropriation is so ubiquitous as to seem like a rite of passage: almost every white pop star has gone through a period where they've borrowed the coolness, exoticism, and aesthetics from Black, Brown, and Asian cultures, only to give it up when it no longer suited them. The rate at which these identities can be tried on and discarded by white people is alarming, but its frequency has numbed us to the impact of cultural appropriation. Our theft is not without consequence.

Many will argue that *all* cultures appropriate each other and are influenced by one another, and that that's what makes our diverse, melting-pot society so rich. But when our unquestionably dominant, white culture takes from cultures we've ritually subordinated, with zero context and giving zero credit, then profits from it, it's not sharing—it's cultural appropriation. This is why, for example, Vietnamese people cannot culturally appropriate American culture. When we've forced non-white citizens to assimilate for their own survival, we cannot call that assimilation cultural appropriation.

Cultural appropriation of Blackness, for example, is a continuation of theft from a community that we've already taken too much from. Ironically, we take from Black culture while harboring deep feelings of anti-Blackness. We cannot call it "appreciation" or "borrowing" when it continues our legacy of stealing from and profiting off Black people and using it for our own livelihood and status, a national practice that goes back to 1619.

When it comes to Blackfishing, we're stealing from a culture that most white people know very little about, and carelessly adopting the styles for which Black women have been punished and discriminated against in a culture that prizes European beauty standards. It gives white people the privilege of shape-shifting at our own whims without recourse, while the

Black and Brown women we're taking from face very real social, professional, and financial consequences for not adapting to the European ideal of beauty. Bias toward natural Black hair, for example, is so prevalent that we need to have policies in place to mitigate against it.

In 2019, the CROWN Act was introduced by Holly Mitchell, a California state senator—*CROWN* standing for Create a Respectful and Open Workplace for Natural Hair.[34] It was the first state law to ban discrimination against natural hairstyles at work or in schools. The NAACP Legal Defense Fund states: "Hair discrimination is rooted in systemic racism, and its purpose is to preserve white spaces. Policies that prohibit natural hairstyles, like afros, braids, bantu knots, and locs, have been used to justify the removal of Black children from classrooms, and Black adults from their employment. With no nationwide legal protections against hair discrimination, Black people are often left to risk facing consequences at school or work for their natural hair or invest time and money to conform to Eurocentric professionalism and beauty standards."[35] We cannot be so casual about trying on Blackness like a costume when Black people are facing penalties at work and in school for wearing their hair naturally, and children, like Yseult as a young girl, feel shame about their features and bodies. We must stop taking from communities to whom we still owe reparations. Black hair culture is one that non–Black people will never really understand, so for us to appropriate it so casually feels like pillaging, especially when you consider that the CROWN Act was only introduced in 2019.

I try not to participate in this harmful trend, but I've absolutely been influenced by it. While the term *Blackfishing* is relatively new and the trend has been popularized by Instagram, the practice isn't. In high school and college in the early 2000s, I

---

34   https://www.oprahdaily.com/life/a30459491/senator-holly-mitchell-hair-discrimination-bill/.

35   https://www.naacpldf.org/natural-hair-discrimination/.

lived at the tanning salon and amped up what I couldn't achieve on the beds with self-tanner. I didn't consider that artificially changing my skin tone to make myself darker was problematic. Whereas people of color are subject to colorism in society that prioritizes whatever is closest to whiteness, white women can experiment with darkening our skin while always having the safety and privileges of whiteness. Beauty brands capitalize on skin tone envy on both ends of the spectrum. Even today, harmful skin-lightening creams are a billion-dollar business for companies like L'Oréal and Unilever in Africa, India, and the Middle East, promoting whiteness as the epitome of beauty.[36]

Women are constantly receiving messages that what we are naturally born with is wrong and not enough, and that our social currency is our beauty and how it's perceived by others. With pressure to turn ourselves from humans into brands on social media, a very specific aesthetic has surfaced, perpetuated by influencers and celebrities. The Kardashians, Rita Ora, and an endless list of others have all been guilty of Blackfishing. Some people might be surprised to know that pop singer Rita Ora, frequent wearer of cornrows and afros, is white. In a radio interview with New York station 105.1, referring to being mistaken for being Black, she said, "I might as well be. I like that. It gets me places."[37] We're far from being in a place where these attitudes should be seen as acceptable. Not that many decades ago, the Black singers who invented the soul music that so many white stars today are influenced by couldn't even stay in the white-owned hotels where they headlined.

A very public case of cultural appropriation surfaced in December 2020, when Twitter user @lenibriscoe tweeted the fol-

---

36 https://www.forbes.com/sites/jemimamcevoy/2020/06/26/loreal-unilever-reassess-skin-lightening-products-but-wont-quit-the-multi-billion-dollar-market/?sh=3d88fbca223a.

37 https://thetab.com/uk/2020/08/11/rita-ora-isnt-black-shes-a-blackfish-and-here-are-the-receipts-170436.

lowing: "You have to admire Hilaria Baldwin's commitment to her decade long grift where she impersonates a Spanish person."[38] The user went on to share videos and articles illuminating us that Hilaria—a yoga instructor, mom influencer, and wife of actor Alec Baldwin—was actually born Hillary, and not in Spain but in Boston. She was a white woman born to white parents with deep roots in New England—who simply grew up vacationing in Spain.

Over the years, rising to prominence after her engagement and wedding to Alec, Hilaria made several media appearances where she spoke with a Spanish accent (on *The Today Show*, in a segment where she's making gazpacho, she reviews the ingredients and says, "How do you say in English? *Cucumber?*") and had appeared on the covers of *Hola!* and *Latina* magazines. There was a flurry of backlash and fury at Hilaria for misleading the public, lying about her origin story, and taking opportunities from actual Latinas. Hilaria did not seem contrite, but rather explained that she had grown up in a "mix of cultures" and didn't expect people to understand.

Aside from the Internet's glee at catching a celebrity in a lie, Hilaria's blatant cultural appropriation of impersonating an immigrant is extremely problematic. Like the Blackfishers, she wants the exoticism and sexiness of being foreign without the realities of hardship.

In bell hooks's 1992 essay "Eating the Other," a piece on cultural appropriation as commodity, she says, "Within commodity culture, ethnicity becomes spice, seasoning that can liven up the dull dish that is mainstream white culture."[39] hooks's view is that "otherness" is something that white people aim to con-

---

38   https://www.vogue.com/article/hilaria-baldwin-accent-controversy-explainer.

39   https://bookshop.org/p/books/black-looks-race-and-representation-bell-hooks/11024029?ean=9781138821552.

sume, either materially or sexually, for our own liberation from the blandness of whiteness.

I'm not calling attention to these examples of white women "seasoning" themselves to demonize them as racists. People are layered, and not the sum of their mistakes. These conversations require nuance and shouldn't be dismissed as identity politics. We can like Rita Ora's music and appreciate Kim Kardashian's work on freeing the wrongfully convicted and still question the impact of them appropriating beauty and culture from women of color, profiting off it, and influencing millions to do the same.

Hopefully, if some of our most famous white celebrities knew they were participating in this form of racism, maybe they'd stop perpetuating these micro- and macro-aggressions. But the phenomenon isn't widely reported by the white media. An editor for a women's magazine shared with me that her publication was reluctant to cover the topic of Blackfishing, since it couldn't really be addressed without pointing to major celebrities like the Kardashians. Their omnipresent influence, and ability to help sell copies and garner clicks, scares editors from publishing anything critical about them, which perpetuates the problem and condones it by omission.

This conversation inevitably sparks a debate about the difference between appreciation and appropriation. Yes, cultures borrow from each other all the time, and none of us are immune to being influenced by what we see popularized in the culture. But the lines do seem pretty clear when, for example, non-Black people are casually playing with hairstyles that Black women can lose (and have lost) their jobs for. Or when white women are photographed on the cover of *Latina* magazine, taking the space of an actual Latinx woman.

It is not just women who Blackfish or culturally appropriate. White men, too, have long had an infatuation with Black culture: from the white rock 'n' roll musicians of the 1960s to white rappers who use the N-word or speak with a "blaccent."

The streetwear and sneaker industry, so heavily influenced by Black culture, is widely white-led. The sneaker resale industry is a multibillion one alone, though few of the popular resale sites are Black-owned, so those who pioneered the styles don't get to share in the profits. Charlie Lahud-Zahner wrote for *Anti-Racism Daily* that "while celebrities like [Billie] Eilish and Eminem can wear baggy clothing without question, others who wear the same outfits risk being stereotyped as 'unprofessional' or 'dangerous.'"[40] It is not appreciation when some groups are penalized for their cultural expression and the borrowers are not.

In "Eating the Other," bell hooks describes cultural commodification as "consumer cannibalism" that demotes and distorts the origins of what we're consuming. hooks's essay is just as relevant today as it was in 1992. Whether it be beauty trends, streetwear, or music—we continue to ignore history, context, and the voices of the people impacted by our rabid consumption.

"To appropriate" is to take without permission. I do believe that so many of the examples that I mentioned weren't based in a malicious intent to steal, but done out of ignorance, a result of the omnipresence of white supremacy. I'm not calling for public shaming, or a round of "canceling." But bringing awareness to the way racism manifests and compounds and how we contribute to it is crucial to being an aspiring ally. Having conversations about why cultural appropriation is problematic isn't necessarily comfortable or black-and-white, if you will, but we should be having them.

---

40 https://the-ard.com/.

TEN

Why the Inner Work
Is So Important

Allyship is an inside job, since it requires relearning and reconditioning so much of what our society has bred us to believe about race, and coming to terms with how we, as individuals, have contributed to a racist society. We need time to reckon with where we're currently at and learn the tools that will help us out in the world. It's not something that we can rush, co-opt, or half-ass if we're serious about our impact.

These are questions that we, as aspiring allies, should ask ourselves: What's my "why" for being an ally? What are the ways I want to contribute to anti-racist work? What have I been blind to? Whom have I hurt with my ignorance, good-intentioned or otherwise?

When I was just beginning to wake up to the white lens, white supremacy, and the way it manifests in every area of our lives, I felt outrage. I wanted to point out every white person's problematic behavior and explain to them why it was wrong. But as I came to realize, calling out other white people is not usually an effective tactic for bringing them into the conversation, and it only distracted me from taking accountability for my *own* problematic behavior. Also, it wasn't my role to position myself as a white savior for *other* white people.

Letting go of old belief systems can be challenging, and I've had my share of what I like to call "fragility flare-ups" as I've evolved. Those flare-ups usually come when I feel compelled to defend myself and those old belief systems, because I'm scared of the anger, hurt, and truth that I'm being confronted with. I'm reminded of an Audre Lorde quote: "The angers between women will not kill us if we can articulate them with precision, if we listen to the content of what is said with at least the same intensity as we defend ourselves against the matter of saying." Her words remind me not to dismiss anger or be scared of it, but to understand and learn from it.

A few years ago at a corporate job, I was called into Human Resources. I assumed that we'd discuss the allyship group that I'd helped start at the company, since we worked closely with HR. Instead, HR informed me that one of my colleagues had reported me for using words like *white people* and *white supremacy* in the workplace, and that my coworkers had found the language inflammatory. Bringing up topics about race and racism while trying to recruit members for our group, it seemed, was not going over well with my white colleagues. At first, I was in disbelief, and then I was outraged at their efforts to silence me. I named all the micro- and macro-aggressions I'd witnessed at work, all the racism that they were perpetuating at the magazine and spreading out to millions of consumers. Their wrongdoing *needed* to be called out, I thought.

The woman I met with in HR, a Black woman, told me that racism was going to happen in the workplace all the time. As an aspiring ally, I had to learn how to communicate and bring people into the cause without alienating them with language they weren't ready for. Yes, it was ridiculous that I was reported to HR for saying "white people," but she was absolutely right about changing my approach.

If the goal was to bring more of my colleagues into anti-racism work, then my outrage and self-righteousness wasn't going to lead to a change in their behavior—just more defensiveness. Also, almost everything that I abhorred about the racism I was seeing in others had been a part of me at some point. While it's important to hold others accountable, the mirror often needs to be turned inward, first.

Being an ally requires a shift in identity and a willingness to look at the ugly parts of ourselves. Before we get to the doing, we must reckon with who we are being. Our egos want praise, to be the best, and see allyship as a ladder of virtue to climb. There won't be a point where we become "fully actualized allies," and allyship is not a "yoga retreat for white people's souls," as Yseult has said.

Some psychologists posit that we reject and judge others for the behavior that we reject and judge in ourselves. Kind of scary, and also humbling, right? The unattractive traits are the ones that we hide and feel shame for the most. Under that philosophy, there is no hierarchy of white allies, since we're all simply reflecting each other.

Know Better, Then Do Better

The inner work sets the foundation for the action, or more visible "outer" work of allyship. Being an ally requires study, just as we would study anything else that's important to us, and the humility to begin under the assumption that we know even less than we think we do. I often feel I have less confidence now than I did when I started this journey years ago, and I don't think that's a bad thing. We don't know what we don't know. Starting an anti-racism journey has required me to completely reeducate myself. Not only are there major gaps in my very Eurocentric education, I've also been taught outright lies.

★ ★ ★

Growing up, I did not learn about the Little Rock Nine, the nine Black students who integrated a white high school in Little Rock, Arkansas, and who faced months of mob violence from students and adults (and at first, with no protection from the government) for the "crime" of trying to get an education while Black. I didn't know anything about this moment in our history until I watched the 1987 documentary series *Eyes on the Prize*. Had I been taught about the Little Rock Nine in school, perhaps I would have recognized how my white privilege granted me an education that I didn't have to face abuse for, and I'd have better context for the education gaps that exist between white students and students of color. Those brave nine children who walked up the steps of their high school with their heads high, despite the vitriol and imminent threat of death around them, might have been my heroes, had I known about them.

I didn't learn about the Great Migration until reading Isabel Wilkerson's *The Warmth of Other Suns*, recommended by one of our podcast guests, journalist Rochelle Ritchie. Wilkerson wrote about the millions of Black people who risked their lives to flee the Jim Crow South, only to be met with more racism in the North—refugees in their own country. That book dispelled any remaining illusions that racism was only a Southern sentiment.

I didn't grasp the trap or impact of the "model minority myth," and how it harms Asian Americans, or know that it was an American doctor in Korea during the Korean War who popularized double-eyelid surgery by experimenting on Korean sex workers and brides of American soldiers, to make them appear more American and "trustworthy," until I read Cathy Park Hong's *Minor Feelings*.

I didn't read the work of Black, queer, feminist writer and activist Audre Lorde, whose work would have altered the lens of my early feminism to be more intersectional, radical, and less racist, until finding her books in a McNally Jackson bookstore in my thirties.

I was unaware of the depth of society's conditioning that told me to hate my body, and that anti-fatness and anti-Blackness were linked, until reading Sonya Renee Taylor's book, *The Body Is Not an Apology*.

I had never truly appreciated my American citizenship or grasped what it was like for immigrant children and adults to live in fear until reading the memoir *Beautiful Country* by Qian Julie Wang, one of our podcast guests, about living undocumented in the United States after moving from China.

I didn't know that our country keeps disabled Americans living in poverty by preventing them from accumulating wealth, because they can't have assets totaling over $2,000 and at the same time receive supplemental security income until we interviewed disability advocate Imani Barbarin on our podcast.

The gaps in my education are like canyons, and you might feel the same. But I can't blame my parents, my teachers, or society for my miseducation now that I'm an adult. A new educational foundation is my responsibility to build. Knowing our history and having context changes our perspectives, and it's necessary to allyship. It is not up to our Black partners or friends of color to sit us down and share this knowledge with us—it's up to us.

A "Woke-Up" Call

Most new aspiring allies make the mistake of focusing first on outward allyship. On a small scale, that might be making a donation to a social justice organization. On a larger scale, maybe it's a company creating scholarships for people of color. We like proof—something that we can point to and say, "See? I'm an ally. I donated this amount of money. I hired this person. I volunteered for this organization." However, if our own internal white supremacy isn't reckoned with, those outward actions won't have a positive impact, and our allyship will have a short shelf life.

I'm reminded of one instance in my life where this was made clear.

A few years ago, when I started the allyship group at my former company, a senior white, Jewish woman was asked by HR to be the group's executive sponsor to support our group and to attend our meetings. I'll call her Susan.

She and I met several times so that I could share with her the goals for the group, and we could decide the cadence and content of the meetings. The group was meant to inspire allyship and cross-racial dialogues at the company, and we met with the Black and LGBTQ affinity groups so that we could bring their feedback and concerns into ours. Affinity groups were new at the company, so we were learning as we went. Susan was a practical, no-nonsense businesswoman, and she seemed enthusiastic about combating racism at our workplace. She shared with me that she'd specifically hired interns of color from her alma mater for years, and it was something she was really proud of. After months of planning with HR, and with Susan on board, we were ready for our first meeting.

At the first gathering, there was a turnout of about ten employees. We did an exercise called "The Privilege Walk,"[41] where participants stand in a horizontal line. During this exercise, the moderator reads lines like, "If you grew up with people of color or working-class people who were servants, maids, gardeners, or babysitters in your home, take one step forward," or "If you grew up in an economically disadvantaged or single-parent home, take one step back." The goal is to visibly see how race, gender, citizenship, education, and income affect our levels of privilege and get us farther (or not) in life.

I took the role of the moderator. Everyone took their steps

---

41   https://www.eiu.edu/eiu1111/Privilege%20Walk%20Exercise-%20Transfer%20Leadership%20Institute-%20Week%204.pdf.

forward and back, and when the walk was finished, participants looked around to observe where they ended up in relation to others. The white and male employees were closer to the front of the room, and the employees of color and women were closer to where they'd started. Everyone seemed to be quietly taking the exercise in, except for Susan.

"I should be farther back," she said, irritably. She seemed unhappy that the exercise had placed her farther ahead of most of the group. It was clear that she felt she'd been more oppressed than she appeared. "I've been discriminated against as a woman and as a Jew," she said. I sympathized with her—knowing she was of a generation where those identifiers hindered her more than they did me. But the uneasy feeling in my stomach was telling me that maybe Susan would be a problem.

After the Privilege Walk, we sat around a table and began a discussion about the differences between the white employees' experiences working at our company and those of the employees of color.

Susan, however, didn't see any discrepancies. She talked about her legacy of hiring interns of color, one of whom had been brought on full-time and was attending the meeting. "You're having a great experience, here, aren't you, Brittany?" (Names have been changed.)

"Um, well…" Brittany said, then went on to share that in fact, she'd experienced microaggressions and other indignities since starting at the company.

Okay, I thought. *Brittany couldn't have been more blunt. Maybe this will be Susan's wake-up call.*

Several employees of color shared similar experiences of having to code-switch or erase parts of their identity to help them get by in a majority-white environment.

As the meeting went on, at one point, I used the word *woke*, then followed it up with a self-deprecating comment about how I knew that that word was overused. The meeting ran about an hour and a half and seemed to go well, if a bit awkward, as expected.

A few days later, I received an email from Susan, saying she wanted to meet with me—I figured she wanted to digest the meeting and plan the next one. I was looking forward to talking with her about the illuminating and vulnerable experiences that had been shared, and how we could work to change the harmful dynamics happening at the company.

But when I walked into her huge office, Susan was livid.

"You embarrassed me!" she told me.

"…What?"

"You made fun of me for saying *woke*! You ridiculed me in front of the whole group!"

I was truly stunned. I couldn't reconcile her accusations and anger with what had occurred at the meeting. I respected her authority and would never consider ridiculing a superior in our place of work. It was like she was accusing me of showing up to work naked—it wouldn't happen. Not only was I stunned at the accusation, I was shocked at her efforts to redirect. Was she honestly making this about her and her feelings? Didn't we have bigger things to discuss? Wasn't she galvanized to keep going? I felt I'd entered an episode of *The Twilight Zone*—a rewrite that centered the most senior, successful white woman as the main character and victim in a meeting about combating racism.

I explained to her that I remembered the meeting differently.

Reminding me of her goodness, she yet again brought up the internship program she'd started and the discrimination she'd faced as a Jewish woman. And then she said, "I don't think I'm the right person to sponsor this group."

I left her office devastated and took the elevators straight to the gym locker room to cry in relative privacy. I felt berated and betrayed, like an elementary school student who'd just been scolded and given a time-out by a teacher for something I hadn't done. Why would she invent something that didn't happen? Had

I just witnessed flaming white fragility? I called several friends who'd attended the meeting to see if they remembered "woke-gate" as she did. Their memory mirrored mine. I had made an offhand comment about using the word myself, and there was never a moment where I implicated Susan.

It seemed like Susan believed, like most of our white colleagues, that getting people of color through the door of our company was enough. She recognized her ability to grant the opportunity, but she didn't recognize her responsibility for the toxic environment that she was bringing these employees *into*. Susan didn't want to do her own inner work, so the meeting triggered something she wasn't willing to see or accept. Before we'd even held the first meeting, it seemed that she'd decided that because of her previous good deeds, she had no further work to do. It was clear from her behavior that she'd wanted to use the meetings to talk about her own oppression, not others'. She barely seemed to hear or have sympathy for her own employees' experiences of racism when it was shared, let alone be able to acknowledge her responsibility in being any part of the problem. Susan made me the bad guy, so allergic to her own discomfort that she invented a reason to excuse herself from the work completely.

I felt disillusioned, but it was a wake-up call for me and my own inner work. I recognized my own naivete for believing that somehow, the sailing would be smooth as I tried to bring others into the conversation, and I'd underestimated white defensiveness getting in the way of allyship. I also realized that I didn't have the skills or words to meet this resistance; instead, I cried in the face of it. I was ill-equipped to be leading these conversations by myself. A new corporate sponsor was assigned, as was an amazing Black coleader, Terrence, to run the meetings with me. We made slow progress, month by month, and created a space that we and the company could be proud of.

Defensiveness is a common reflex in white people, especially us white women, whenever the subject of race is broached. Because we understand the oppression of being female, we often unfairly equate it to the oppression of racism, or oppression of those who live at the intersection of oppression, racism, and any other "ism." In our effort to find common ground, we draw false equivalencies that only highlight our lack of true understanding. It's best for us to listen and validate people of color when they share their experiences and allow space around those vocalizations without jumping in with what we might see as our similar experience of oppression.

If we don't learn to manage our defensive impulses, we don't have much hope for bridging the gaps. When we can't sit with the discomfort, we're likely to opt out and remove ourselves from the conversation completely, like Susan did.

Had Susan been more willing to listen and not react with defensiveness, her participation in the group could have had a huge impact on its success, the experiences of non-white employees, and the company at large. We would have leaned on her to recruit more senior members of the company to our meetings, and to bring the dialogue to different teams. She might have brought the anti-racism conversation into her personal spaces, creating a ripple effect beyond the company. We also wouldn't have had to spend time and resources placating her and finding her replacement.

The inner work of confronting our victimhood, white savior complexes, and denial isn't comfortable, but it's the most crucial part of our allyship journey.

I had mixed feelings bringing up the notion of "inner work" in this book because I worried people might have a connotation of it being "woo-woo"—like yoga, veganism, or meditation. I want white people in particular to understand that there's something major to gain by doing this work: your humanity! Not just for me or those like me, even if secretly I wish for a better world for my future children. The real reward comes to those who know they are making the world a better, more equitable, less dangerous place for their fellow humans. If that's not a goal worth pursuing, I don't know what is.

When I thought about what it would take for things to change, I had to come to peace that it wasn't just a case of white people knowing the difference between right and wrong. I had to accept that even the most intentional white folks will at some point say something racist, problematic, and definitely triggering. It's not a reality that's easy to verbalize out loud, because I'm terrified that white people will use this as an excuse. Yes, white people in a white supremacist society are tainted in how they see the world, how they understand people, and how they view themselves in cross-racial dynamics, because white supremacy isn't a thought or feeling. It has managed to systematically insert itself in absolutely everything that is part of our society.

Take the concept of a Karen: an entitled middle-aged white woman who is aggressively racist and all too happy to provoke a situation that can become very dangerous and potentially lethal for BIPOC involved. Karens are the result of white supremacy, but they're a hundred percent at fault for thinking the way they do, because there's enough information for a Karen to be different and better. She's the direct by-product of her environment, upbringing, and societal conditioning that reinforces her voice and her feelings about other people's business and lives as superior to others'.

I'm apprehensive writing this because of white people potentially saying "OMG, look—it's not my fault!" Simultaneously, I could anger the BIPOC community, who might feel like I'm giving excuses. The reality is that it's not a specific individual's fault, but it is a white person's obligation to address white supremacy and unlearn it so that they don't continue to uphold the legacy of segregation and violence toward nonwhite people. There's so much more work to be done on an individual level to break the cycle. There's no other way to end white supremacy but to actively act against it by getting out of the box society has created to maintain it.

The Interpersonal Approach to Restoring Humanity

The way I see it is, it's up to white people to make lasting change, and that starts on an individual level—at home, and in everything that you are involved with. Often the responsibility to make the world more equitable is put on BIPOC communities, and white supremacy wants us to believe that the person harmed, aggressed against, and violated has to be the bigger person and work on fixing the dynamic. With all due respect and love, I say, "Fuck that." The only way for our culture to change is for Lindsey and Brad to start seeing that they are feeding into a mechanism that hurts me, those I love, and everyone on the off-white spectrum. White people must stop feeding into the energy of shrugging their shoulders or pointing their fingers at others who are visibly more problematic.

Let's investigate two major ways racism manifests, using home-buying as an example.

A *macro level* of racism is when Black people don't have the freedom to move to their chosen neighborhood due to practices like redlining, where cities and towns installed rules over the years to limit the ability of Black people, and POC in general, to live where they want.

In the *micro level* example, we'll use Joe from New Jersey who's decided to become a real estate agent. He probably didn't think to investigate racism in the real estate industry and what BIPOC families experience or feel when they are in the process of looking for a home. Joe may not know, which doesn't make him racist inherently, but if he's upholding toxic behaviors that are feeding the machine of white supremacy,

Joe is now actively part of the issue and he's continuing the legacy of racism in real estate.

It's not his fault that when studying real estate there weren't classes on racism, but it's his responsibility to read and educate himself so he's not perpetuating harm in his field. These issues are well-known within the BIPOC community; they're not isolated incidents. If Joe took the time to connect with BIPOC communities, he would learn about the deep roots of racism within his industry. Most Joes won't look into macro issues and will understandably try to "fit in" and be like other people in their field. In a space that's mostly white with no outside insight, I'd bet it's a toxic one.

Joe's responsibility in this situation is to take steps to unlearn the norms and get to know the toxic history so that he can better understand the BIPOC families that he might work with. By doing the work and questioning the "norm," he's now moving forward and participating in restoring humanity in himself and his industry. He's on his way to becoming an ally.

If I'm still not making sense, I think the best example is when women complain that men aren't our allies—that they're nice and all, but a lot of the time they don't do due diligence to see how they may be contributing to sexism. Yes, women aren't treated well and we are still fighting for basic rights, but on a micro level men have to take time to listen and see how they are participating. Are they joining in on toxic masculinity behaviors and thoughts? Are they laughing at a friend that's being super touchy when a girl said no multiple times? Are they calling in their problematic male friends to help them change? Are they advising their women friends when they have creepy friends so they can be safe?

Yes, the macro level is that we live in a patriarchal society that upholds toxic masculinity, but how are men individually taking a stance and making a difference? I am willing to give space for growth and change, but I don't think that time alone changes anything. It just erases memories and makes people think systemic issues happened long ago, and since they're not obvious, they don't exist anymore.

What white people need to understand is that when it comes to interior work, we are all vessels for our ancestors, and if we don't purposefully untangle and let go of the things that are part of the past, racism will never die. Otherwise, my children will go to school with your children and experience the same mess that I had to go through, and that's just not something that sits well on my heart.

We can't go back and undo what was done, but I expect and demand accountability to not reproduce what your mothers, uncles, and grandparents have done. There's power in breaking cycles for the better. It restores the humanity that white supremacy robs you of and also makes life better for us.

I once had someone tell me that by looking at things in an interpersonal way, I'd never end racism. First off, I don't dare give that to myself as a goal. There are so many levels to racism, and so many different communities are fighting their own individual battles. I don't represent all of them and wouldn't have the expertise to speak for them. I also really believe that BIPOC shouldn't be the ones wanting to end racism. It should be a collaboration between all of us who care to make the change.

I believe that there are many ways to go about addressing racism, and in every endeavor, there are amazingly talented people giving their time and energy to help with the problem. Addressing it interpersonally—like through friendships—is something that feels attainable to me. I also believe that all movements of change begin with people, shoulder to shoulder, forced to reexamine what we have been doing and the impact each and every one of us has in this matter, starting with well-intentioned white friends and peers in our lives.

I think going the interpersonal route allows people to see

the difference they're making as they apply their allyship. I can't tell you the gratification I feel when a Kinswomen student or client gives us the feedback that they have seen and felt a difference in their lives. I feel even more joy when BIPOC come to us and say that they feel more comfortable in whatever environment they're in where others received training. It's those moments where I see that the interpersonal work we do has a real and tangible impact.

We are all connected, and we all have power. From parents raising kids and having a say in their local school, to the doctor becoming aware of the racial issues within medicine, to the real estate agent learning about redlining. All these people are linked to a community and have the ability to have a positive impact. I want to see white people embracing this.

Think of it this way—there's not enough money I could make or degrees that I could acquire to protect my future or my children. The only way for me to be in a more comfortable and safe space is if white people from all backgrounds do the work to be the aware and compassionate teachers, police officers, lawyers, doctors, delivery people, and all the other types of humans that I come into contact with on a daily basis. Each of these interactions is casual and minimal, but have an impact that we don't tend to acknowledge.

I realize that it may at times seem scary to be on a path to allyship, but it's extremely rare for white activists to be hunted and killed because they are supporting and advocating for BIPOC and other minorities. One rare instance is the infamous freedom fighters, Andrew Goodman and Mickey Schwerner, both American Jews who were assassinated alongside James Chaney, a Black American, fighting for civil rights in 1964 in Mississippi. They were murdered at the hands of the KKK. It is interesting to note that half of the white allies to the freedom fighters of the Civil Rights Movement were Jewish, something I feel isn't shared and spoken about as much I wish it would be.[42] If more people knew, I think it would help unite people in their continued efforts to eradicate racism against visible minorities and Jewish victims of antisemitism today in America. Historically, this fight for equality happened together and can again.

I've seen firsthand how a conversation and taking responsibility can have a big impact. My friend Becky, a white American woman, decided to look into her own involvement and impact when people started protesting and marching for Black Lives Matter in the midst of COVID. She was a friend and I knew she supported me personally and was familiar with my work. She is a more than decent human being, and has a wonderful husband and three boys, who are all white. At some point she realized that she wanted to be proactive, that having a good heart and intentions wasn't enough, and that she wanted to do something within her community. She gathered people to create an initiative in her town, a predominantly white space.

They started the Haddon Township Equity Initiative, made of nine mothers who wanted to make their mostly white town a place more equitable to live and grow up in, and not just for white families. They started by digging into the legacy of their town and soon realized that the closet was full of racist skeletons. (Which, let's be real, is the story of the whole US of A.) I love to share her story because she genuinely wanted to make a difference. They did this as a group of white women, not to be performative for BIPOC around them, but because they wanted to understand the legacy of their town and make a real difference. Together, they created a space for conversations and to address the town's history of white supremacy, which wants to hide and bury itself deep in the soil. With bad soil, nothing healthy can be grown.

It's not easy looking at where we are from, especially if it's

---

42   https://rac.org/issues/civil-rights-voting-rights/brief-history-jews-and-civil-rights-movement-1960s.

not as pretty and great as you were told it was. I was brought up by my mother to always remember where I'm from. It's something I never forget, and I work hard to uphold my family's legacy and bring us into the spaces we belong. For a white American, I can see why you wouldn't want to look at where you came from, but acknowledging the past, as ugly as it may look, is the only way to prevent history from continually being dragged through the gutter, and from the barbarism that social injustice creates. I don't want any white readers to think I'm trying to shame anyone; rather I'm pushing you to embrace all that you are so that you have a better idea of who you want to be and the impact that you choose to have.

The inner work is so hard because it requires you to look at parts of yourself that you didn't have control over but that exist and have to be acknowledged. It feels like we have to take ownership of other people's actions that happened before we were born, but knowledge is really the key to sustainable growth and genuine change.

I don't want to normalize minorities laying down their lives to make a difference anymore. That's not the only way to bring about change. I don't want people to die like MLK and Malcolm X anymore. I don't want prayers and posts. I need to see white people unlearning and becoming useful in this fight for justice. I want the conversation about BIPOC in the West to be focused on humanity and our contribution, not solely based on the pillage and violence we have experienced.

I heard it from His Excellency Paul Kagame, president of Rwanda, that we can aim for big pictures and goals, but it's the little things that add up and make a real difference. I couldn't agree more, and it feels especially relevant to the work in this journey of true and genuine allyship.

ELEVEN

Allyship in Action

I have my personal guess as to why white people have a hard time taking action on their journey toward being an ally. The idea of being an ally is appealing, and the social rewards are enticing, but the actual process to be a genuine and intentional ally isn't glamorous. Allyship isn't something you do for the glory, but for the sake of humanity.

I know we often talk about how white people need to give something up, either monetarily, or the comfort and privilege that comes from being white or white-passing. Frankly, I think donating money or services is the easiest part of allyship. The way I see a white person be a real ally is by being purposeful everywhere they exist and in everything they love, especially when there are no BIPOC to witness their allyship. This requires so much more intentional analysis and action. It's intense to have to examine the world we deem "normal," and to admit that certain realities that you've accepted as real are false.

YSEULT P. MUKANTABANA & HANNAH SUMMERHILL

The Truman Show Effect

When Hannah and I first started the conversations that would lead to *Kinswomen*, I was ready to hear the worst from people, even from people who seemed normal and *are* good in many aspects of their lives. They could be my coworkers and potentially even my friends. We offered a space that gave white people a chance to be themselves, without holding back. I always entered our conversations with these women chanting to my heart that this is for the greater good and that they at least are showing up. Also, I would make sure my heart had a little cushion for the cringeworthy comments and remarks that were sure to come from our dear guests. It's challenging and strange to be in a room with people that you know want to be better but in the process are so harmful. I just made sure to make it about them and their journey rather than myself.

In college, I studied and dissected movies and other media for my communication degree, and my favorite classes were with Dr. Sheena Howard. I took all the subjects I could with her; she was ruthlessly strict with her work, but it was in her classes that I picked up the bug to analyze all the media that I consumed. She was such an inspiration. Dr. Howard encouraged us to dissect everything around us, which helped me understand the world better and as a result, fear it less. (My communication degree is coming to full use, professionally and personally, to be honest.)

One of the films we watched together was *The Truman Show*, a 1998 movie that stars Jim Carrey. He plays Truman, who's adopted at birth by a film production company, and while his whole life seems normal, he actually grows up and lives on a film set. In this made-up, pristine town, every single person is a hired actor, so that Truman never finds out that everything that he has been experiencing isn't real, but a show that's broadcasted to millions.

220

Truman falls in love with a woman who happens to be part of a movement of people from the outside world; she also falls in love with Truman and wants him to be free from this fake world. He starts to sense that his life is scripted, and he goes on an emotional journey where he struggles to make sense of everything.

His whole life, Truman had never tried to leave the island where his town was located because there was a traumatic, choreographed moment of his "father" dying in the sea. Until now, he had been petrified of the ocean.

After the production team and the director of the show attempt to stop him, they give up because they realize he's reaching the wall that determined the end of the set. His boat smashes into it, and he realizes that his whole life was an indoor production. Truman then arrives at a door that everyone watching is waiting for him to walk through, and that's when his "father"—who's really the director—speaks. He asks Truman, "Do you really want to join a world that isn't perfect, where I can't protect you from harm like I have here?" Truman steps out into the real world, and that's the end of the show and the movie.

This movie is from the late '90s, and I remember it making a big impression on me. Like, how could a person be so sheltered and exist in such a boring world? I always felt like I would have picked up on it! There's no way I wouldn't have known.

Now as an adult, I'm deep in a space of parallel realities and basically work with people who are the Trumans of their own little world. White people that are nice people and not aggressively racist are typically the individuals that we have in our spaces with Kinswomen, through our community gathering and our consultations. They come in with a varied spectrum of blindness and awareness—some may know more and others are completely new to these conversations; I welcome them all the same.

During our conversations, there are dramatic revelations

and discomfort that frightens white people. Some freeze and stay quiet because they're overwhelmed, while others will speak up because they want to process the choke out loud. Some let their discomfort manifest in defensiveness. All of these reactions are common and predictable; it's like watching a play and knowing the ending without even having seen it before.

One commonality with all these people is that they can't unhear what they are told. They can go back to their lives and continue living the way they always have, but they've heard some truth they won't soon forget. I think many people don't want to be in a space of hearing these truths because it's worse when you know and don't do anything than being in complete ignorance.

Like Truman, there's no way back to what life was before you realized how racism works. You can't go back to unseeing the devastating truths that affect your friends every day. The storm Truman battles trying to reach beyond the island is white folks battling with guilt and discomfort, because there's a lot to process realizing that your ignorance made you be part of the problem, even if you are a good person at heart. The door Truman took to exit that fake world—filled with lies meant to numb his mind of reality—is the step aspiring allies must be willing to take to make lasting change in their lives.

There's no sequel to *The Truman Show*, but I can guess that Truman would struggle with adapting to a world that isn't familiar, and he would have to find a community that understands him and is willing to teach him. When white folks want to make a change and be part of the solution and not perpetuate white supremacy, they need community and resources, especially early on in their journey.

Walking through that door isn't easy. But it's the surest way to reestablish the humanity that white supremacist ideology has robbed us of in white spaces.

Illusion of Loss

White supremacy wants you to think that there's loss in being an ally, to keep you passively maintaining the status quo and harming BIPOC. There's no loss of life or livelihood when you become an ally, rather a letting go of something you are familiar and comfortable with.

One way that white people do this is by claiming that racism no longer exists. It's wild to me when I meet a white person that looks me dead in my eyes and tells me, "Things have changed and racism doesn't exist anymore." They go on to list some of the most successful token Black and POC, like pointing out that Oprah is superrich, or bringing up Jay-Z and Beyoncé, to support their claim. I eye roll while they painfully realize that their discomfort in the conversation is taking over, and they are being problematic. As we've said before, acknowledging racism and identifying where it exists is the only way we can move forward.

The craziest part is that some people see whiteness as a culture, which it's not. Culture isn't violence. Culture is a collection of achievements from a specific place and people including food, dance, clothes, rituals, arts, and so on. American culture isn't the legacy of white supremacy even if that's how the American nation came to exist. American culture is the richness of the diverse elements and people that make it relevant in the world. Intellectuals from around the world come to the US, and even if they are from Brown or Black countries, they strongly reinforce the nation's strength. I must remind everyone that Albert Einstein was a Jewish man running away from European genocide. He was a German Jew. The irony—and what breaks my heart—is the number of antisemitic attacks and how antisemitism has found its way into schools, politics, and everyday violence. I cannot for the life of me accept that the US is where such things happen, when diversity has always been the pillar and backbone of this country.

Despite what white people may fear, there's never been a movement of BIPOC wanting to reciprocate what white supremacy has done. There's been nothing remotely close to the barbarism of colonization, segregation, Jim Crow–era laws, physical violence, mental violence, displacement, rape, slavery, or anything else white supremacy has enacted upon Black or Indigenous people done to white people in America. I think because America was built on the backs of the enslaved Africans and the murder of Indigenous nations, there's this constant fear specific to the US that one day the Black and Brown people will rise and hold authority over white people. This is such an impossibility, as every law and the constitution itself were created to make sure that could never happen.

I think white supremacy does an amazing job at vilifying BIPOC and communities advocating for BIPOC rights as something that's meant to hurt white people. The best course of action when I am really scared about something is to rationalize it as much as possible. That's why I always call for information, not to counter or fight, but to look at something as objectively as possible. If white people did the same, they'd see that the fight against white supremacy is really the fight for freedom, equity, and a better life. There's no intent to kill or to do to white people what has been done to BIPOC. Everything that the Civil Rights Movement had to fight for benefited more than just Black American society. Everyone benefits from a more free and equitable country.

Seeing conversations of reparations and allyship finally start to happen gives me a little solace and glimpse of hope, like when light hits your poorly lit and overpriced New York apartment; it makes you feel like maybe things are going to get better. Is there anything better than accountability? I think it's a universal language of love that white nations and people need to prioritize when they aim to change things.

BIPOC aren't the only ones who will prosper from change.

Personally, it feels good and liberating when Yom Kippur rolls up and we are told to ask for forgiveness and make peace with those we may have caused harm. I mean, it doesn't feel comfortable to take responsibility, but discomfort doesn't kill, and the outcome is freeing and lays the groundwork for genuine conversations and support.

I want to be honest about things and make the most contribution that I can to these conversations, because it keeps me sane. It keeps my heart light and reminds me of my humanity.

My Feelings About Allyship

It's frustrating and reminds me how deeply entrenched white supremacy is when a white person asks me how to be a good ally. No one asks someone else how to be an environmentalist or an advocate for animal rights, and I know we wouldn't be asking those questions even if plants and animals could speak. We inherently know that it's not just about caring about animals or the environment, but taking actions that positively impact their existence. More than we're willing to admit, we do know how to turn caring into action.

But when it comes to anti-racist work, I still have to convince people that my life and the lives of people who look like me are worth fighting for—how upsetting is that? I have to make sure white people don't feel attacked when we have conversations about race even when it's people like me who are actually experiencing harm. I am still confused when we get questions like "Where do I start?" You have to start right there in your home, at your job, when you go grocery shopping, and with your family.

Allyship in action is going to feel like learning to ride a bike or doing anything for the first time *all the time*, because there are levels to racism and by-products of racism that come up when you are in this space—you're going to be wrong at times and make mistakes, but you have to be ready to hear from the group that you're trying to be an ally to.

Writing this reminds me of a story of a white female ally who started a movement in her town for the Black community. The white woman decided to take a stand for her Black neighbors, but she ignored the very community she was "trying" to support when they said they weren't comfortable with how she went about her support—to the point where the Black community explained that they felt unsafe with her approach.

The white woman didn't get it, and she claimed that the Black community needed to stop acting scared and take a stand. She felt like she was doing something to help (save) them and wasn't willing to hear out the people concerned, because her heroism had taken over her willingness to understand. Her ego blinded her from being an ally. Instead, she alienated the community, and they were *really* upset. If you aren't willing to hear the people or community you're wanting to support when it comes to their comfort and safety, you aren't an ally.

We could consider a similar situation but as a dynamic between women and men. Imagine if a guy had one of their female friends experience sexual assault from a male individual. The guy friend decides to stand up for their friend and bring justice, which, as an idea, is great. But if he doesn't ask his friend first, to see if she feels comfortable with the action he wants to take before he does, it's like taking away agency from the person that's concerned, causing another layer of trauma. A conversation has to happen before he can use his privilege best to support her in her experience. He cannot decide what to do because only she will have the insight to know how he can help her.

BIPOC often want the same kind of consideration from white allies. I've seen many situations where white people feel offended that they can't just freely run to "help." It's not because BIPOC don't want allyship; it's because it shows a lack of humility in recognizing that you do not know the best for other people just because you come from a place of privilege.

Ideally, the process for anyone who wants to be an ally to any community, really, is learning about the issues, then turning to the community that's the closest as an anchor in your journey. Hold yourself accountable to the people you care about and find those willing to talk about the issues outside of your own community. And finally, take actionable steps to apply what you learned in your own spaces daily.

I like to imagine that allyship is really about having a good relationship with your friends. The love and labor that we pour in friendship is what genuine allyship feels like; it must fit and calibrate to each specific friendship you have, and you must be able to hear and make space for those that you care about so there's a respectful interaction. Applied and genuine allyship provides the tools to know better about what's happening in the world and to your friends, and ultimately gives you the stamina you need to stay alert and not fall into a space of doing nothing.

From Awareness to Action

Sometimes it takes one aha moment, like Truman, to see through the lies and bring white supremacy into clearer focus. In our work, we've seen that once our students come through our courses, they're excited to bring allyship into their spaces. The white lens has shifted, and they want to share what they know with others. Maybe now that you're nearing the end of this book, you feel energized about what you've learned or unlearned, and you're ready to make some changes. If so, amazing! But here's what you might find: living our values can be harder in practice than in theory, and moving them from brain to body will take time.

Knowledge to embodiment hasn't been easy for me, and I

struggle and often make mistakes along my journey to allyship. I've pointed the finger outward when it should have been facing inward, I've centered myself, and I've put energy where it was wasted or wasn't meant to go. It's an ongoing process to internalize the values I say I align with. We may believe that we're already living according to our values, but we act, often subconsciously, in ways that prove otherwise. As aspiring allies, we should be asking ourselves how to bring integrity to every area of our lives.

I love the liberatory consciousness framework that Dr. Barbara J. Love, an author, activist, and organizational transformation specialist, has developed for aspiring liberation workers to move from awareness to action and allyship. A liberatory consciousness, she says, allows people to "…live their lives in oppressive systems and institutions with awareness and intentionality, rather than on the basis of the socialization to which they have been subjected."[43] This framework recognizes that we have all been socialized to behave in harmful ways and in oppressive systems, but we do not have to be helpless or hopeless about it—there are steps we can take to liberate ourselves and others.

The first step toward allyship is **awareness**, and hopefully, your antenna is more sensitive now that you're nearing the end of this book. Awareness is when we're able to recognize racism in the thoughts, behaviors, and actions of ourselves and others instead of denying it. It's removing the white lens and seeing and accepting the harm that's happening. Initially, it might involve pointing out problematic incidents to others. I spent a lot of time in this space, mistaking it for actual allyship—I'd call people out on social media, at work, or in my family. That wasn't necessarily effective; rather, it alienated people and fed

---

43   https://d31kydh6n6r5j5.cloudfront.net/uploads/sites/574/2020/10/dev_liberatory_conscious_001.pdf.

my ego. Be mindful of self-righteousness as you continue this work. Awareness is one of the most important steps, and a lot of people never get there. But we can't just be aware and do nothing about that awareness—which leads us to the next step in the liberatory consciousness framework:

Analysis. After gaining awareness, we can start to analyze and ask *why*. It's "interrogating what we see happening in the world around us from a liberatory perspective."[44] Instead of just being able to recognize inequity, we question why it exists, how it happened, who it benefits. We may become aware of the larger structures of systemic racism at work. It's going beyond saying, "The team/cast/company is mostly white and it's problematic," and asking why and how those dynamics came to be.

When I read books like *The New Jim Crow* and *The Color of Law*, it helped me analyze *why* there was so much disparity in the prison population, and segregation in housing and school systems. Education and conversation help to deepen our analysis and understanding of the structures we participate in. Analysis then leads to:

Accountability. If we're serious about allyship, then we must be accountable to those whom we wish to be an ally, and be willing to hear and take valuable feedback so that we can be better allies. This work isn't about receiving praise for our good deeds. Instead, it's about being humbly part of the solution, and it's important that we acknowledge and support one another when our "internalized domination and internalized subordination manifests itself in our lives, and agree with each other that we will act to interrupt it."[45]

---

44 https://www.barbarajlove.com/.

45 https://d31kydh6n6r5j5.cloudfront.net/uploads/sites/574/2020/10/dev_liberatory_conscious_001.pdf.

★ ★ ★

Finally: **Action and Allyship**. This is the step that many aspiring allies are eager to get to: the *doing*. We wouldn't run a marathon, or even a 5K, without training first. Dr. Love says that action can include: taking individual initiative, organizing and supporting other people, or providing resources for others to take action.[46] The first steps are crucial so that we can take action that matters.

While it may feel slow or clunky at first, moving through this process again and again will become more fluid. You might be overwhelmed, because when you begin to gain awareness, you realize that there's racism everywhere, in everything. So start small.

We can begin with ourselves and bring awareness to how we're spending our time and money. Who are we giving those assets to? What kinds of media and information are we letting consume our time, and how does it affect our worldview? Analyze, then take accountability and action. We can challenge ourselves to allocate those valuable assets in a way that supports the causes that we believe in. Look at your monthly calendar and expenses. Can you increase the percentage of those assets that go to BIPOC-owned companies and organizations?

When it comes to your friendships, take an honest inventory of the closest people in your life. Do they all identify similarly? Ask yourself why. If you have friends who identify differently, how close are those relationships? Analyze: When's the last time you shared a meaningful conversation about their experience? Is your friendship one that feels safe and liberatory for both of you? Then, accountability: What's our responsibility in this dynamic? What does the other person need from us? Take action

---

46 https://d31kydh6n6r5j5.cloudfront.net/uploads/sites/574/2020/10/dev_liberatory_conscious_001.pdf.

toward allyship by implementing the four tenets of trust, and taking the feedback from your friends to heart.

After looking at your personal life, consider how to use this framework in your professional life. Awareness might mean noticing the diversity (or lack thereof) of the employees at your company. Analysis is questioning why: Why have BIPOC left the company? Is hiring bias at play? Who are the leaders making the decisions? What's the workplace culture, and how have I contributed to it?

Accountability then might be taking responsibility for the culture and determining what our roles are in making changes. Action and allyship could look like reviewing systems like hiring and annual reviews, hiring a third-party DEI (diversity, equity, and inclusion) consulting group to conduct surveys and lead sessions, and establishing a culture code.

I know that while these steps may seem simple, in reality we might feel terrified if it's up to us to implement them. Maybe we've been working on reeducating ourselves for months or years, but when it comes to bringing this new, more aware self into the real world and having conversations about race, we falter. We feel awkward asking our friends of color at work how we can support them. We don't challenge our in-laws when they make a comment about "Black-on-Black" crime. We lack the bravery to challenge the landlord who makes a comment about only leasing to "the right kind of people."

Questioning the status quo, speaking up, and facing ostracization for doing so is not easy, especially for new aspiring allies. You might even mourn your old self—the one who lived comfortably and naively under the white lens. If you are white, the reality is that it's a safety net that we can always fall back on. Your new self might feel like a radical departure from the old you.

My life looks completely different since starting *Kinswomen*. This work has profoundly changed and challenged me, forcing me to ask myself why I'm here on this planet at this point in time.

It's demanded that I get clear on my negative and positive impact, which has inspired more honesty and truth in my relationships. I can't and won't turn back.

Being an aspiring ally is not only recognizing the privileges that we have, but putting that privilege to work. The more you use your voice and your privilege, the more confident you'll become.

I was out with friends recently and the bartender asked the three of us what our jobs were. He had no follow-up commentary about my friends' careers as lawyers, but after sharing with him what *Kinswomen* was about, he seemed somewhat challenged by my mention of anti-racism. "I'm color-blind," he said. "I smile at people in the street and I'm not an asshole. It's that simple."

Five years ago, I probably wouldn't have said anything in response, not wanting to disrupt the levity of the evening. Or up until a few years ago, I probably would have chastised him for calling himself "color-blind," which wouldn't have yielded a productive conversation. Instead, I saw the moment as an opportunity for a dialogue. Though he was defensive at first, we ended up having a broader conversation about allyship and activism, what our individual responsibilities were, and we learned from each other.

We disagreed on several points, and I didn't leave the interaction feeling satisfied exactly—it was awkward to discuss racism with a man who'd just served us peach cobbler, and these conversations do not end with a cherry on top. But there are no perfect answers, and warm and fuzzy agreements won't often be the end result. If we begin conversations about race wanting to avoid mess, we're missing the point, which is to unravel and question all of our assumptions and dogma around race and racism, and leave room for nuance, disagreement, and growth.

If you're white, maybe what I described feels risky to you: making waves at work, speaking up to strangers. But allyship in action requires risk from us as white people. Most of the time, the only real risk is our comfort, which is not a risk at all. As Yseult said earlier in this chapter, yes, it might feel like we are giving something up. But what is *really* at stake? The lives and liberation of our friends and fellow citizens, who risk *a lot more* when they themselves engage in activism.

For me, it's been helpful to reframe what risk and fear look like when it comes to activism. It motivates me when I learn about the Little Rock Nine, the Freedom Riders, the Ferguson protesters—they faced real risks to their lives, and yet they took direct action anyway. Maybe it felt like their only choice. As a white woman, I will never know what that feels like.

One example of allyship in action is from a fashion designer named Laura Harrington, a white friend of ours who owns the vintage brand Fly By Night. She's intentionally made anti-racism part of her brand by offering resources prominently on her website, donating proceeds from her sales to anti-racist causes, and being transparent about her own allyship journey on social media. It's become such an integrated part of her business that other fashion designers have asked her to help them incorporate their values into their brands, too. Yes, she's also lost some customers by being transparent about her mission, but she's inspired others. Taking a stand *will* alienate some people, but that is a risk that we must willingly take.

One of our Kinswomen programs, the Course for Anti-Racist Entrepreneurs, challenges business owners to consider how their lens impacts their business: the kinds of employees and customers they're attracting; whether their brand is actually inclusive; and how their branding, marketing, and hiring can either support or hinder the values they purport to uphold. Our students' biggest fears are losing customers or facing resistance from their audience. We share with them that we cannot believe that in speaking up about justice, we only lose. We ask them to consider the customers and clients who might be waiting to hear the company articulate their values, the peers they will inspire, and the ripple effect that they could have in their community.

Amplify the Activists Already Doing the Work

It's sobering to recognize that while I may have recently woken up to the injustices surrounding us, others have been fighting those injustices for centuries. We can maximize those efforts by contributing to the organizations that already exist. Sometimes it will be up to you to be the leader in your community, like Becky, who started a justice organization in her all-white town. But before you lead, do your research to discover who's already doing the work, and learn and take guidance from them.

For example, if you believe in reparations, the repayment to Black and minority communities for centuries of disenfranchisement and stolen labor, find out if there's a larger organization currently leading the charge that aligns with your values. I'm a member of the Fund for Reparations NOW! (FFRN!). It's the white ally initiative of the National African American Reparations Commission, who guides the organization. I make monthly donations and attend meetings on the status of the HR-40 bill (the Commission to Study and Develop Reparation Proposals for African Americans Act), first introduced in 1989.

Recreating the wheel and starting my own reparations organization based on my passion alone would have been a distraction from the larger mission. The experts deserve our support, and they're typically the ones most impacted by what they're working for or against. We can then use our voice and platform to direct attention, energy, and funds to amplify those efforts.

Whether it's combating medical bias, prison reform, or the intersection of environmental and racial justice, there are leaders in practically every field where racism exists doing important work that needs our support.

TWELVE

Coming up Against Resistance—
In Yourself and Others

Preparing for Resistance

You might have read the last chapter and thought: "Absolutely not. No, Hannah. I am not about to risk my time, energy, or friends for this." I can relate if you're feeling fear and resistance to the idea of allyship in action. That's normal—when we're on the precipice of change, we want to stay where we're comfortable because it feels safe. Not only will you feel internal resistance to allyship, you'll face resistance from others, so this chapter is meant to prepare you for resistance to the Resistance, if you will.

Resistance arises from our fear of change and the unknown. As white people, we are unaccustomed to having candid conversations on race, much less admitting culpability and participating in reparative action. Conversations on race and responsibility can feel like we're ripping up the social contracts that require people (especially women) to be forever polite and accommodating and to keep conversations in light and neutral territory. So in breaking from that, you might feel queasy, vulnerable, or terrified when you come up against resistance in response—I know that I often did, as I share later in this chapter. Disrupting the status quo will feel radical, but in actuality, it's not radical—it's bare minimum. Yseult articulated this brilliantly when she said, "There is absolutely no glory in being a decent human being."

At times, we come up against resistance even when a situation, on the surface, seems supportive. I'm reminded of a consultation Yseult and I had with a white-male-owned coworking space. A female employee reached out to us, excited to work together. She wanted us to be interviewed for a piece for International Women's Month; specifically, how white women could be allies to women of color. Great. Their mission sounded like it aligned with ours. They were going to publish the interview on the company's blog, as well as sponsor a giveaway where the winner got to work with us, and they agreed to pay us $500 for the session with the winner. We'd made it clear our partnership needed to have a monetary exchange. They agreed.

Later, the company decided to scrap the giveaway, but keep the interview. After being sent a long list of questions asking us how employers could close the pay gap, we were told we wouldn't be paid, due to "the ethics of journalism." The irony of rescinding the opportunity for payment while expecting us to lend our voices to a piece about Equal Pay Day and closing the pay gap was infuriating. (Also, do employers need our advice to close the wage gap? Can't they just…close it?)

Yes, we understand journalistic ethics and the industry standard for not paying for interviews. But we will not lend our intellectual property or faces to a company who only wants to *appear* as if they're doing meaningful work, but not actually allotting value or resources in the form of financial compensation. In short, we will not support performative allyship.

And maybe our journalistic "ethics" should be reconsidered. One of the four guiding principles of journalistic ethics, for example, is to minimize harm, according to the Society of Professional Journalists.[47] Isn't it harmful that women are expected to work for free, especially when talking about closing the gender gap? Another principle, according to the SPJ's site, is to Act Independently, and "deny favored treatment to advertisers." I can attest from a decade of working in advertising sales at magazines that this rule gets broken every day. These principles are well-intentioned and extremely important, but only if they're wielded for good, decided upon by a diverse range of journalists, and not bullshit. Does it seem radical to challenge the rules of journalism? It kind of does. But any system that undermines the value of women of color and white women does not seem ethical, which is the point we were trying to get across to the interviewer. We never ended up partnering with them.

Recently, I posted the statistics of the gender and race pay gaps, along with a real-life example, on my Instagram. The numbers are unacceptable: White women earn 78 cents for every white man's dollar. Black women earn 61 cents. Hispanic/Latinx women earn 53 cents. Asian women earn 91 cents.[48] Native women earn 60 cents.[49]

Sometimes, we forget there are people behind the statistics. When I worked in media, many of my friends of color shared their salaries with me. Though we'd had similar education and years of experience, in some cases I was making more than twice what they were.

After I shared the stats on Instagram, several BIPOC replied to my stories saying that they'd been on the low end of the wage

---

47   https://www.spj.org/ethicscode.asp.

48   https://www.businessinsider.com/gender-wage-pay-gap-charts-2017-3#overall-black-and-hispanic-women-face-the-biggest-pay-gap-when-comparing-earnings-to-non-hispanic-white-men-4.

49   https://leanin.org/data-about-the-gender-pay-gap-for-native-american-women#!.

gaps at work, too. But several white followers reacted with resistance, responding with the equivalent of, "Yeah, but..." and making excuses for the salary disparities or sharing that they were also underpaid at work.

Sigh: the resistance and the cognitive dissonance. Even with statistics and real-life examples, we have an impulse to resist reality. If you ask most people, they'd say that they don't want their own bias to negatively (or positively) impact what other people deserve to earn, or to get in the way of what they themselves deserve. They'd also likely say that they don't want to work in a place where bias and racism exist, and that if they could close the wage gaps, they would.

But I think the reason why white people want to deny the reality of the wage gaps is because admitting so would mean having awareness that there is a problem, and then we'd have a responsibility to act after gaining that awareness.

We so badly want to believe in meritocracy that we will resist evidence that proves that it's a myth. We want to believe that we, and those in charge, are not susceptible to bias when it comes to hiring, promoting, deciding salaries, and giving bonuses. But if we deny the facts after seeing them—the hard data, plus the personal stories—we are guilty of maintaining inequity, and the wage gap is likely to only get wider.

The resistance I faced on Instagram, from white people whom I love and respect, is not surprising, nor is it uncommon. You are likely to face similar resistance even when you're armed with the facts.

You may face resistance coming from within. When I first learned about the event at The Wing where I met Yseult in January 2019, I was looking forward to it. But when the day came, I was tired from a long day of work, and told my husband I wasn't up to trek to Brooklyn for the conversation. "You've been looking forward to it. You should go," my husband said. I realized that he was right—I'd RSVP'd and made a commitment to attend. I was feeling resistance to putting myself in an unfamiliar and potentially uncomfortable situation. I'm so grateful for that push Dave gave me, because if I hadn't gone, my life would look so different than it does now.

There's a reason we start off all of our classes and workshops with a disclaimer that discomfort and resistance is normal. Even though the participants sign up with good intentions, sometimes our students attend one class and aren't heard from again. Or they register, give us their money, and never show up. Our good intentions without follow-through is just a performance.

Know that you *will* face resistance when you are asking or being asked uncomfortable questions—but don't let it knock you off course.

Resistance from Powerful People

If we find speaking up on social media intimidating, speaking truth face-to-face to those in powerful positions may feel impossible. In having conversations about race, especially with someone in a position of power, we might freeze, shut down, or be silenced when they respond or challenge us and we realize that we don't have the precise answers. You might be able to identify that something is problematic and wrong, but you don't yet know how to articulate why or contribute to a solution. As you move from awareness to analysis, outlined in the previous chapter, in time you'll be able to respond with more clarity in the moment. It's also perfectly fine to say, "I don't have the exact answer right now, but these are important conversations that deserve more time and energy." As white people, having productive conversations comes with practice.

The president of my former company used to host monthly breakfasts where we'd get the opportunity for face time and to ask him questions. It was his way of making himself seem human and accessible, I suppose, and they were coveted invitations. When I attended one of these breakfasts, everyone sat quietly around a conference table, politely sipping their coffee. As we went around the room to introduce ourselves and pose questions, I asked what his plans were when it came to DEI at our company. My last company had recently been bought by this one, so the DEI conversations I'd had with the previous HR team collapsed with the sale of the company as most of the team was laid off. Now, at this breakfast, I had the opportunity to go right to the top. I was scared, sweating, to ask him about this in front of my boss and colleagues in attendance. But why? It was just a question, and a valid one.

After I asked my question, the president leaned back, crossed his arms, and delivered a mildly defensive nonanswer about how hiring initiatives take time and effort, recruiting diverse candidates was hard, and to just have patience. Wait and see, wait and see, he said.

It wasn't a satisfying or concrete response, but I hadn't thought through my follow-up question, so I didn't ask one. The conversation was over. Today, I would have asked about what else the company had planned to do outside of hiring. Maybe we could have brainstormed ideas about doing an all-staff DEI training or doing paid feedback sessions from the employees of color who already worked at the company to improve their experience. All of those efforts might have helped to make the company more attractive and sustainable for future employees of color.

Not only was I facing resistance in myself to ask the question, I faced resistance from the president to take the issue of DEI seriously at our company. Because I wasn't prepared for it, the opportunity for a wider discussion about inequity was lost. As a woman who didn't experience racism at the company, I'm sure I wasn't the first to bring it up. Likely, HR had dozens of complaints or suggestions from current and former employees of color about what needed to change. But our president resisted these truths, until it was too late, and the racial reckoning of 2020 came around. He resigned from the company shortly after, amid various allegations of misconduct. Real leaders lean into the uncomfortable truths, own up to their shortcomings, and take a proactive approach toward progress.

The resistance you face in your work toward allyship might be a source of pain, disappointment, fear, or defeat. Leaning on your friends and your community is necessary for leverage and support. Even if you feel alone, know that your people exist. Your community, even if it's only a few people, even if it's only *one* other person, will keep you from backing down out of fear or intimidation.

Friction in Close Relationships

In a post–November 2016 world, so many of us experienced fissures and fractures in family and friend groups due to Trump's election, an event that revealed the fundamental differences that exist in our close relationships. Many members of our community found themselves in stalemates with their parents, their partners, or their friends, wrecked over the gaps in values they couldn't seem to bridge. Conversations with those closest to us can be the hardest and most emotional to have.

I've had conversations with family and longtime friends—almost always people who consider themselves to be on the liberal, "open-minded," "non-racist" side of things—that have left me dejected and disillusioned. However, these conversations are far more productive than arguing with strangers on Facebook. With those we know best, we most likely know the best ways to reach them. I know my mom loves to read, so a few years ago, I took a more passive approach to calling her in and gave her a copy of *So You Want to Talk About Race* by Ijeoma Oluo. She was hesitant at first, but she read it. In the years since, she's become a frequent attendee of our workshops and classes, and is doing her own activism with food banks in Pennsylvania. I'm so proud of her. In between then and now, there's been discomfort and tears as we each worked through our own defenses, both often feeling righteous that we were good, well-intended white women.

Similarly, on one episode of our podcast, we discussed a trip to a plantation I'd planned while in Charleston for a bachelorette party many years ago. Yseult wanted to talk about the topic of plantation weddings. As she rightly pointed out, it was a macabre American tradition for white people to celebrate love in such a barbaric place. I wanted to share my journey from naivete to regret about this particular trip. It wasn't until after I came home and spoke to my husband about our trip to the plantation and hearing his feelings about it that I realized how clueless I'd been. "It's as if you're dancing on tombs," Yseult said on the episode.

On the podcast, I expressed remorse and responsibility for ignorantly planning and participating in a racist, "Southern belle" antebellum fantasy of visiting a plantation. I was a fan of the Bravo show *Southern Charm*, set in Charleston, which glossed over the city's racist history and had a cast that at the time was absent of Black people. That was the version of Charleston that I'd come to see and wanted to visit.

My friends felt like I'd attacked their character on our podcast, even though I meant to share my own personal experience and reflection on the trip. In hindsight, I wish I would have had the one-on-one conversations about the trip with them before speaking about it on a public forum. If I want to call people in, they can't feel blindsided.

I was surprised and heartbroken to encounter resistance in my close friendships, and I didn't feel prepared for it. I was resisting the hard truth that as I change, so will my relationships, and not necessarily in ways that I expected.

Questions to consider:

- **Is there a conversation you've been putting off, or an action that you've procrastinated taking?**

- **What issues or topics in this book do you feel resistance to?**

- **Where do you think your resistance comes from? What is it protecting?**

Moving Past Resistance

When it comes to resistance that arises from conversations about race, I've seen how it manifests in a physical way, like a rubber band. When you stretch it hard it can snap at you, unless you release it gently. And the more tightly you pull on the rubber band and create resistance, the bigger chance it has of snapping and hurting you, which is why I always flinch when I'm interacting with someone who is clearly stretched thin.

I think that with anything that's uncomfortable, it's always hard to lean in. The inherent step we want to take is back, which tightens the rubber band. I've been working on trying to remember that embracing discomfort can be so freeing, because it gives space for growth, change, and deep soul liberation. I have seen it work in the most amazing ways when white people work through the discomfort that comes from their own resistance.

I want this work we do with *Kinswomen* to be focused on white women, because the resistance of white women to make these much-needed changes has hurt BIPOC more than we would like to believe or admit. Women carry the legacy of a nation; I believe that. White women carry the culture and legacy of whiteness they inherited, and if they're not conscious of the weight and implications of that, they carry it into their communities and their families.

They hold privilege and power that they should accept and put to use to help others; the way they vote, the way they raise their children. White women have a seat at the table that isn't equal to white men, but they are in rooms that most BIPOC don't even have access to. This privilege should be seen as a powerful tool that can make a huge positive impact in the lives of people of color!

The feminist movement does not have an innocuous history and has often focused solely on the rights of cisgender white women. The first feminist movement in the US was led by white women who wanted voting rights for themselves but not for BIPOC women. It's these layers that make conversations across races so important. I need white women to understand that the silent and compliant behavior isn't proper or cute—it's patriarchy working to make sure you don't feel obliged to speak up for yourself or anyone else, and to see BIPOC women advocating for themselves as a loud and problematic thing.

I don't want white women to read this as an accusation or me singling them out. Rather, I wish there was more of an awareness of how white women can use their influence and privilege as a tool to bring the change we need. I don't want this conversation to get muddied by seeing this as a gendered attack; this isn't a "catfight," but a realistic look at who is able to do what in our fight for equality given white women's access. This is a reminder that white women have power to make things better, and my sincere hope is that they will.

Holding on to Long-Term Resistance

As we approach old age and become more physically vulnerable, our conscience has a way of creeping up on us, and our brains have a way of reminding us of things we have deeply buried. All of the resistance, ignorance, and harm we've caused in our lives are things we ultimately must confront. I don't wish this on anyone, and I live my life trying to make sure that I don't end up regretting that I didn't do more.

I recently read a story a nurse told on social media about an old lady she tended to. The nurse explained that this woman was dying from COVID-19 and was scared and hallucinating. At some point, the old lady told the nurse that she saw a little Black boy in the corner of the room, but there was nobody there. On her deathbed, the woman then asked the nurse if she could confess something, and the nurse accepted.

The old woman then went on to tell her something that had happened when she was a little girl. She had been jealous of two little Black sisters from her school; she felt that they had prettier dresses. Then she said that she wanted the little Black girls to feel bad, so she went to tell her white parents that their brother had touched her behind the store. After this lie, the system ran its course. The boy was taken by racist adults, he was hung, and his genitalia cut off. This act of violence on Black boys and men was done because in the Bible it's written that a man without genitalia doesn't get to access paradise, and they wanted to make sure the little boy's family knew that the child couldn't even reach peace in death. The men also burned the family's home, so they had to run away while mourning their son, all because of one little white girl who was jealous of a dress.

The woman, now on her deathbed, confessed her lie for the first time ever. I was so shocked by this story that I had to share it with my mother. She reminded me that all the little white girl did at the time was get jealous and tell a lie. It's the system and the adults who really committed the barbaric actions. These are wise words that gave me space for compassion for this old woman and prevented my heart from burning up from the sadness and anger that rose up from hearing this story.

And it's true, the little girl didn't have the maturity or perspective to understand the tragedy she caused. What did trouble me, however, is that she was telling this story *now*, dying, because she was eaten up by the fear of death, not guilt, which could have made her try to do something, anything, to make it right. Even if there's no realistic way she could have made it right to the family she had caused harm to, maybe she'd have become someone that advocated against racism and she'd have told this story earlier. I don't have the answer as to how a person makes amends for something like that. My brain tries to find logic in something that it can't. Even though I really wanted to be angry and hate the woman, I felt pure sadness that this story was her legacy, that this poor Black family had no chance or voice against a white child's words. It's not the first story I've read like this, and it won't be the last one, but my heart still aches.

There are many stories like this. Humans using their power and taking advantage of the defaults and norms that hurt others; in this case, a Black boy that had done nothing wrong was killed, his family tortured, and their lives ruined.

These are the kinds of stories white people need to reflect on, lean into, but not because I want them to feel guilty or horrible for something that isn't necessarily directly linked to them. I want these stories to remind us that the system in place permits these horrific acts against BIPOC. There's an urgent need to do something, through leaning in, accepting the past, and seeing how they can make a change in their schools and communities.

I think white people would like to think that change is going to happen on its own, that eventually someone else is going to do the work and things will be fine, like when an accident happens on the highway and people pass by without calling for help thinking that someone else will. We cannot bet on luck. The resistance to learning from these kinds of stories holds us back from a better world. Everyone should feel a call-to-action, because that first step is necessary for a road to a better future.

It's still hard for me to grapple with white resistance when I'm confronted with it. I continue to feel hurt and surprised.

But I never want to stop being affected and disconnect from my feelings. The day I trivialize horrid events done to BIPOC or trivialize people resisting and not caring is the day I will not be able to speak on these things ever again. My softness is my strength, and my vulnerability is the only way I am able to look at things differently and not be nurtured by the rage I feel.

There's a limit to how much resistance a white person can have to learning and trying to do better. At some point, when someone has all the information and has been invited to have conversations and they still are resisting, as a Black person, I choose to learn to let go. I cannot bear the thought that someone would hear what is going on in this world and think they can opt out of doing anything. I believe in healthy boundaries and ending relationships that don't hold the same values as I do. I hold more space for family because those relationships are more complicated, and you should have more love for your siblings and parents. But if you think the environment is toxic, it's okay to take a break or just distance yourself completely—from friends or family.

We have had white people in our community gatherings, environments that are more relaxed and low-key, that have expressed that they are afraid to lose their white friends that just don't hold the same type of spirit. Don't get me wrong and think I want you to dump your dearest friends. I want you to know that it's a valid option to consider. Just like when you go vegan or if you love hiking and being outdoorsy, you want friends that reflect these values and mindsets. You'll also make new friends in the new spaces you'll occupy and, little by little, your friend group will better reflect who you have become and what you believe in now.

THIRTEEN
Welcome to the Beginning

I want all BIPOC and Jewish people to feel seen and heard through this book. I hope this comes through as a love letter to them. I want BIPOC to feel like a main character and feel represented in these pages. As a Black woman, my story isn't one of oppression but rather of thriving in the midst of daily insanity; it's a story that focuses on holding on to a glimpse of humanity in the midst of darkness.

It's also an homage to my little self, flown in from Burundi at age five, landing in a country and culture that questioned and erased aspects of myself before I even realized I held them in me. I wanted to speak on my experience as a whole person and human. I've found there's power in taking up space where people aren't used to seeing people like you. This book is to claim space for people like me, a story based on my observations and sentiments. I want this book to be a starting place for those leaning into their discomfort to have solace that there are others like you.

I was told by my mother early on, "You have to know where

you are from to know where you're going." This phrase has evolved into something that I apply and see differently today than when I first heard it. I used to understand it to mean that I should never forget that I'm from Rwanda and born in Burundi. My understanding of this was superficial and was limited only to the "where you're from" part. I had never really taken the time to know what she meant by the second part.

As I came to sit in my truth more and accept my layered upbringing and identities, I relinquished the need to have to choose, because I am all of these things: Rwandan, born in Burundi, grew up in Brussels, and living and thriving in the US. The phrase took on a new meaning after reflection. I know now that I must know where I'm from so I can carry those truths and values to where I am going. I don't have to erase, shy away, or compartmentalize, because I can use all that is part of me to move forward with confidence and insight.

I'd suggest white people do the same—know where you came from to know where you're going. It doesn't have to be based on your geography, but more so about your history. America as a nation, and white Americans in particular, want to focus on all the good that has happened, but it's important to know how the good came to be and to whose detriment. There's a parallel reality that makes BIPOC-identifying people live with the looming truth that things haven't changed enough. I speak to this often, and I have decided to do advocacy because America is a relatively young nation that has made a lot of changes in a "short" amount of time.

In this country's existence, so much of it was lived in slavery, segregation, and Jim Crow–era laws, and still today America hasn't moved past this period, because there are people alive who have experienced this all-too-recent past. To a certain extent, things have just shifted to target BIPOC communities in different ways, like the prison system that holds mostly Black and Brown people while they're the minorities in the country.

All these truths shouldn't discourage white people from learning and addressing these issues. We are all interconnected, and if you do better, things get better for all of us. As much as BIPOC advocacy has accomplished, this work cannot be done without the majority in power.

Racism is complex and layered, but I believe in love, in truths, saying the hard things in order to get to a better place. I want to know if I have hurt someone, so I can apologize and understand. I feel pain, and I want white people to know that they have the ability to make real change for others. I want BIPOC and white people to feel empowered by our words: for BIPOC to be seen in a narrative that doesn't pin us down to a story filled with sorrow and despair, and for white people to be empowered to revisit their taught history with a critical eye, eradicate the harmful narratives and education, restore the humanity needed, and change for the better within their own space.

I want us to care about these things in a sustainable and organic way, not only when those from BIPOC, Jewish, or other communities are hurting. I want people to care when we are thriving and succeeding, to normalize and unify cultures around our shared human experiences and vulnerability.

I hope this book gives a sense of permission to white people hesitant to engage when they may be feeling blocked because of unrealistic ideals. The goal isn't to find the magic potion and fix everything at once; that shouldn't be anyone's intention, as wonderful as it sounds.

In my opinion, the greatest way to go about this work is starting where you can and where you feel like you can be vulnerable, and for many people this means in their friendships. I think that setting ourselves up for successful and genuine relationships is the ultimate goal and that begins when we get open and honest with ourselves and invite friends in to do the same.

Perfection Is Toxic

Trying to achieve perfection in this space and in these conversations is a toxic idea and a lie. It doesn't exist, and it makes things stay the way they are. I hope that this book brings light to subjects and perspectives that will help us get closer in our interracial relationships. I hope that it helps make the uncomfortable bearable. My greatest hope is that it contributes to repairing friendships that have been broken. I also hope that minorities feel seen and understood, because I know that it can be hard to find words to articulate these dynamics.

Perfection is funny, because logically, you'd think that it would mean people are working hard and really getting involved. But what I've found is that for the most part perfection frustrates, makes people bitter, or freezes them exactly where they are, afraid that they'll make a mistake. It reminds me of the lava games I played as a child, where we bounded from cushion to cushion so as not to touch the floor. There were two types of players—the ones that quickly jumped all over and the ones that barely moved because they were terrified they might touch the lava. They ended up making the game unenjoyable and missed the point entirely. I'm not trying to say working toward racial equality is like a game. What I mean is that if you stay in your corner and are more afraid of making a mistake than being part of a movement, you're not doing it right.

Perfection makes no sense in terms of self-love and patience— it dictates from a point of view that doesn't incorporate the layers that this work requires, for yourself and others. That's why when I see that white people police and criticize each other on social media about "who has done better," I find it silly and annoying. The person criticizing most definitely is going to get things wrong and is still navigating and understanding. No one has a cookie to hand out to the "most woke" white person, because it's a constant learning process.

I also want to be transparent about this—the distance that gives me space to engage in these conversations and interactions comes from the work I do on myself to process all the problematic things I experience. I wouldn't want anyone who identifies as BIPOC to feel like they owe anything to any white person, or for white people to expect guidance from BIPOC that they don't know. That's why it's important to find a like-minded community that's willing to hold space.

Allowing space to breathe and let go of perfectionism is one of the most important things I've done for myself. I couldn't possibly be perfect at this, and I alone am not able to fix much. I struggle with my own stuff, and I still need time and places where I can go and just exist. I am not impermeable to any of this; I just find ways to restore my soul.

As I shared earlier, I traveled to Rwanda during COVID in November 2020. I love being home, and this time I discovered a deep sense of restoration and peace. I had promised myself that I would come back to Kigali to finish this book, but I didn't realize that this promise to myself came from a deep need in my soul to be somewhere where I felt an inherent sense of belonging, restoration, and love. This was the first visit where I stayed as long as I did.

I had the chance to work at Atelier, a magnificent creative center where I was able to write, surrounded by nature, nestled in the coolest part of Kigali, Rwanda, a country with a thousand hills and possibility. My time there was bliss and a privilege, a place that reminded me of my grandmother and the legacy I was able to create for us.

I now understand profoundly why someone like my mother couldn't stay in the West for longer than a certain amount of time. There's not much that can mimic that feeling of being home. Being there has helped me let go of the idea of perfection and it's given me space to look at my truths, the ones where I am the main character of my story, and also its storyteller.

Friendship & Anti-Racism

I often get asked "how to be anti-racist," which I find silly because there are so many people already being excellent examples who have been speaking up for decades. In its simplest terms, it's just like being a good friend.

Like friendship, it's about boundaries, trust, vulnerability, and giving space for growth. Being an anti-racist is not about saving the world and becoming the patron saint of anti-racism, but bringing back an element that seems to escape these big conversations: that BIPOC deserve to live a life that isn't about decoding whiteness, coping with aggression and attacks, and constantly fighting to be the center of our own narratives and legacy.

No one is perfect at this. People have to be open and willing to give emotional space for others. This applies anywhere people experience oppression.

I do have certain expectations of how I need my friends to show up. I need them to be able to listen and trust that my truth is real and not meant to create discomfort in them. I need my friends to hold space to let me vent and just talk through my feelings, because that's an important kind of freedom.

At times as a white person you will mess up, say or do something to hurt your BIPOC friends. In those moments, it's crucial that you just hear us out, because the combativeness is like hot sauce on an already spicy meal. If we are friends, I expect that you have signed the invisible contract of our interracial friendship that states, in bold font, that you will accept accountability and have compassion, because these can be contentious situations. I was told once that I needed to be more patient because I'd decided to be close to a white person, but I reject that idea, because as much as I decided to be friends, a white person has to consciously decide, too, and know that there will be moments they have to take responsibility and put their ego away.

Let's be honest: friendships are complex. We are vulnerable, and we let our inner child be at play with our friends and loved ones. I say yes to that experience and also NO! I have learned to be cautious throughout the years, because there's baggage and triggers that aren't possible to leave at the door. Otherwise, I feel like I'm falling from a really high building of disappointment when something comes up.

I'm lucky to be able to write this book with Hannah; she's an amazing friend and is continually open to listening when she messes up. Our friendship is not perfect, and there have been moments when her defensiveness is hard to deal with. But she has the intention of wanting to do better and has accepted that being an anti-racist is an ongoing journey.

For my part of the friendship contract, I have agreed to give more space and patience. (Keep in mind, there's small print that says I don't have to do anything that doesn't align with my mental and emotional well-being.) Sometimes our friendship gets taxing and annoying, and there are moments where I just want time away. But our foundation is that we understand each other, and the good outweighs the weird. Plus, Hannah is funny.

Interracial friendships and unions are difficult for me not because I don't like white people, but because they come with baggage I can't carry—for my sanity and emotional well-being. Like all worthy relationships, there are ups and downs—but nothing that good therapy, conversation, and prayers can't fix.

I'm happy that the '90s depiction of interracial relationships can be challenged and that finally we can let go of the idea that because people are having mixed babies, the world is a better place. I used to be one of those people that loved seeing a brand's commercial with all types of people, and get excited because I held on to the mediocre crumbs that white supremacy likes to throw at us so that we don't fuss for more.

Now I understand that mixed babies are great, and to a certain extent are a manifestation that people are following their hearts, but it doesn't predict what these children and BIPOC in these relationships will experience. That is where we need to put our energy, to make sure that the soil in which their individual lives are planted is primed for real and sustainable growth and a thriving existence.

I'm grateful for my friends, the ones that remind me I'm human; that's where I find the strength and belief that everything is going to be alright.

Closing the Gaps

There is no arrival to being an ally, and I say that humbly, knowing that I will be forever on this journey. As Yseult mentioned, there is no perfect way to be one either. I've had to repeatedly remind myself of these truths as I wrote this book, often terrified at how my words might land, and constantly aware of the privilege that I have to write them in the first place. I know that I am opening myself up to criticism and accountability from all perspectives on the ideological spectrum, but I also know that for me silence is not an option. Silence about injustice, silence about what I'm doing about it, and silence about my own responsibility only contribute to further mistrust, inequity, and violence.

I can't offer concrete solutions or expertise, just my own perspectives, which have been informed by the BIPOC educators, activists, and friends that I've learned from. I can share the mistakes I've made (and continue to make) so that white readers, hopefully, can learn a little faster than I did. I recognize that all of us are complex people living in a complicated world, and if you find yourself in the white population, know that when I aim to recognize the humanity in underrepresented groups, I am not

256

dehumanizing you. There is so much magic, life, truth, and progress we deny ourselves living in a white-oriented society. I hurt for the pain caused and also the joy lost.

Certain superficial signifiers might make white people feel like we've made decent progress toward a post-racial society, but they're not enough. If anything, they mask the trauma and open wounds that we need to heal. I hope through this book you've been inspired to look under the surface of interracial friendships, relatively diverse workplaces, and other spaces you frequent, and understand what your role is in closing the wage, health, wealth, and education gaps that we've created. Understanding these gaps means acknowledging the pain, subversiveness, and violence of white supremacy, and recognizing how we perpetuate it in our lives, including in our friendships.

The relationship between Yseult and me evolves and grows day by day. Sometimes I feel like I messed up irreparably, or that our differences will never be bridged, like I'll never really understand her point of view, or she won't understand mine. And sometimes, I feel as if we've made progress in closing the gaps, and I'm so grateful that we've healed one small wound of white supremacy. I don't know if the gaps can ever be closed, but I won't stop trying. What I do know is that I'm forever grateful to have her in my life; it's so much better with her in it.

I want for white readers to close this book and not feel like their work is done, but rather they're inspired to keep digging deeper. Our goal is that this book helps inspire more consistent and honest cross-racial dialogues and friendships, so that all parties feel like they can exist in a place of truth and experience the deep fulfillment of being seen. Interracial conversations and relationships *are* complex and can be messy. By sharing transparently the realities of our own friendship—the love, the awkwardness, the pain, the hope, the confusion—I hope that our readers aim for deeper and more curious relationships where the good and the bad can exist together. If it feels radical or scary for you to start having these conversations with friends in your life, it means that they are important.

Lifelong Accountability

In our lifetimes, it is unlikely we'll see a truly equitable and just society, so we have to stay energized, accountable, and consistent in making progress before the next generation works toward the same. Conversations on race and racial justice will be ever evolving as our society changes and we change with it. As white people, we must continue to listen to the experts with humility and receptivity.

To be accountable to this work, I believe you have to have a strong "why." As I mentioned, I was first inspired toward allyship after meeting my husband, but now, my why is so much bigger than just him. I do this work to right the wrongs of my own actions, and those of my ancestors. I do this for my future children, for Yseult's, and for yours. Under the perceived comfort of white supremacy, white people need to spark the fire to engage us against our own complacency, which inevitably will creep in.

I know that expecting constant outrage from white people isn't realistic, and we've proven to ourselves that it's unsustainable (please see 2020's activism boom and bust). But if we integrate allyship into our daily lives, and it's not an all-or-nothing proposition, we'll be able to contribute regular, genuine, effective action that will lead to progress.

We have so much more agency than our white supremacist, capitalist, and patriarchal society would like us to believe that we do. Our participation is required, and our actions—and inaction—have a larger impact than we might realize. Each day, we're either upholding or disrupting the status quo.

Thinking about my own journey, one conversation with Yseult led to our living room sessions, which led to our podcast and dialogues that I've been forever changed by, which led to this book. I'm grateful that we've been able to reach so many, and I'm grateful for the ripple effect of *their* actions.

To be in this space, I know that it's imperative that I stay accountable to the communities I desire to be an ally to, and to stay accountable to myself. As I've mentioned throughout this book, I've written an allyship mission statement that helps keep me accountable. It reads:

> I vow to do the internal and external work of anti-racism and social justice daily. To uncover, undo, and be honest with myself and others about the realities of the conditioning of white supremacy, even when it feels uncomfortable or inconvenient. I promise to devote at least thirty minutes of education every day on anti-racism. I promise to hold myself accountable. I promise to be brave and push my boundaries in using my voice. I acknowledge that I will mess up, feel confused, feel shame, but I will not let those emotions get in the way of doing this work, which I feel is work of the highest truth, service, and love.

These words may change with time, but they've guided me when I felt resistance, shame, or fear. I encourage you, too, to write an allyship mission statement to keep you focused and prevent overwhelm and distraction. Place it somewhere you can see it, and let it evolve as you do.

Just as Yseult and I gathered our friends and family members in small living rooms across New York, you can do the same in your own communities. Finding a group to support and guide us through allyship is so crucial to our longevity. While I have faith in the impact of individual action, I also know that allyship does not happen alone. Lean on your community and friendships to encourage consistency and confidence, especially when you find yourself feeling alone or ostracized by those who are resistant. I've needed my community as a sounding board, support system, and mirror to my blind spots when I've felt lost, wrecked, fragile, or like I was living in the upside-down world.

On our journeys toward allyship, we have to be open to nuance and make space for contradiction. Our expectation that one person can speak for or represent all is so minimizing to the collective, but as white people, we have a tendency to make monoliths of the other. I grow when I learn from a range of diverse opinions, not just those that are convenient and reinforce the narratives that I'm comfortable with. It's important that we examine our resistance and regularly step outside of our comfort zones, so we can become familiar with the discomfort we'll inevitably be faced with.

When Yseult challenges me on my word choices in this book, or my ideas for social posts or newsletters, or my speech, I'm uncomfortable. Hosting the candid conversations in my living room was uncomfortable. But I didn't let my discomfort eclipse the very important messages that were being transmitted, and the learning and growth that came from it, even if at first I felt resistance. Ask yourself: What is truly being threatened? And what is there to gain from facing my discomfort?

The media portrays racial injustice as having ebbs and flows, but I encourage us to reject the idea that because things sometimes appear "fine" that we can opt in and out of awareness, action, and accountability. We have to question what we aren't seeing and *why* we're choosing not to. What's just past our white lens?

My husband tells me about feeling like his engine is always revved, even if he's walking through a park, constantly aware of how he might be perceived, but the average bystander doesn't see that—I often don't see it either. The same way that our eyes can only take in what's in front of us and parts of our periphery, we cannot know what we're not seeing unless we set an intention to broaden our scope, and be willing to see the perspectives of others. I thank my husband, Yseult, and all my friends, educators, and communities for helping me see what I couldn't or didn't initially want to.

Distance from whiteness should not determine one's health, wealth, life span, or legacy. The more we as white people work to fill in the gaps of our education, have candid conversations about race and racism, and give space for hard truths, the sooner we will bridge the gaps in our interracial friendships and relationships, heal our trauma, and contribute to our society's evolution. I hope we've energized you for the journey, and that you feel prepared to talk about race.

Thank you for witnessing me in my ongoing work toward allyship, something I'll be forever aiming toward. Fellow white people, I hope that you'll join me. Let's promise to get familiar with discomfort, dismantle our white lenses, be willing to hear and speak the truth, and take action as we learn and grow. All my gratitude to Yseult for being my partner in this work.

My wish for you is that you find your own kinswomen.

★ ★ ★ ★ ★

FURTHER READING GUIDE

We hope you feel inspired to continue your reading after finishing this book. Here are some of our recommendations:

Exceptional Places to Start

So You Want to Talk About Race by Ijeoma Oluo

Me and White Supremacy by Layla F. Saad

"Developing a Liberatory Consciousness" by Barbara J. Love

Vital Historical Context

The New Jim Crow by Michelle Alexander

The Warmth of Other Suns by Isabel Wilkerson

The Color of Law by Richard Rothstein

Caste by Isabel Wilkerson

Women, Race & Class by Angela Y. Davis

Feminism and Culture

"Eating the Other" by bell hooks

Sister Outsider by Audre Lorde

White Negroes by Lauren Michele Jackson

The Body Is Not an Apology by Sonya Renee Taylor

"Demarginalizing the Intersection of Race and Sex: A Black Feminist Critique of Antidiscrimination Doctrine, Feminist Theory and Antiracist Politics" by Kimberlé Crenshaw

Essays and Memoirs

Minor Feelings by Cathy Park Hong

Beautiful Country by Qian Julie Wang

I'm Still Here by Austin Channing Brown

Guides and How-Tos

Becoming Abolitionists by Derecka Purnell

Radical Friendship by Kate Johnson

We Should All Be Millionaires by Rachel Rodgers

ACKNOWLEDGMENTS

I am grateful for all the voices of BIPOC before me that gave me the strength to speak my truth unapologetically! Those that remind me that my humanity deserves to be protected and uplifted.

I am thankful for the community and friends that acted like a cozy winter comforter while I wrote this book. Everyone around really came together in a compassionate and loving way, which gave me the strength and inner peace I needed to cowrite our book. My belief that I am who I am because of community came to life while on this journey! I felt safe and nurtured in Kigali; Atelier specifically opened its door in a way that was unexpected. At the heart of the busy city I sat every day at a big communal table made from the trees of my country; every time I looked up a native bird would be singing almost to soothe my heart. While I had local caffeinated tea boosting me, the trees overlooking my stressed and pressed self always provided a shaded space for me to pray when I felt overwhelmed and needed a break. Sandra Kabongoyi Kyoshabire and Amin made sure that I would be welcomed in as family in their space; I felt it and it inspired me.

I also can't thank my parents enough, for both encouraging and supporting me in my professional and personal growth. My batteries of energy were recharged at every end of the day with scrumptious dinners, shared with old and new friends; my biggest blessing was to disconnect and be comforted in my humanity.

This book wouldn't be possible if our publishing house Park Row didn't think it was worthy to share with the world. I am grateful for our editor, Laura Brown. She supported and advocated for our authenticity, which is something that I carry close to my heart. I really appreciate the dedication and presence of our agent, Tess Callero. She was able to really support us in our vision. I am happy that I was able to experience this with Hannah, my writing partner and friend. I hope that our voices will help guide people that read us.

Spiritually I felt supported and guided through the presence of Hashem and the beautifully uplifting conversations I had and continue to have with my rabbi April Davis!

Through this work I confirmed that my mind and my heart are all in sync with my soul and that I will be alright! I want to acknowledge that for myself.

I am so grateful to the early kinswomen who showed up, shared their souls, and made those first living room sessions what they were: Sandy, Frankie, Audrey, Christine, Sharday, Victoria, Yliana, Ellie, Marissa, Jess, Tess, Norma, Nora, Kellie, Katie, Sarah, and of course, Yseult. Thank you—those conversations changed me, and Kinswomen wouldn't be possible without you.

Every single one of our podcast guests has left an indelible impact on me. Thank you for sharing your stories. There are so many who have supported Kinswomen behind the scenes, too: David Walters, Ginni Saraswati, Natalie Lum-Tai, Ismelka

Gomez, Tasha Brandt, and each person who helped us grow and spread our message.

Thank you to my parents, Lisa and Kerry, for the love and the writing lessons. My sisters, Ariel and Mattea—I love you both so much, and I try to make you proud! Grandma Rosie, thank you for reminding me of the privilege it is to write this book. My heart is full from the support and enthusiasm from my incredible, ever-growing family of aunts, uncles, cousins, and in-laws. I know there are so many family members supporting me from the other side, too.

Dave, thank you for taking the veil off my eyes, and for being an epic partner to me each day for the past decade. I love you more than I ever knew I was capable.

I have so much appreciation for the friends who supported me throughout the course of this book, and all the insecurity, fear, and imposter syndrome that came with it—your encouragement gave me the strength to keeping writing.

The Universe sent us an amazing agent in Tess Callero—our brilliant advocate. And to our editor, Laura Brown, and the Park Row team—thank you for believing in our book and our message!

I owe so much to Yseult, for always revealing to me a new perspective, pushing me to look deeper and be better, and for making me laugh. Thank you for being my partner on this journey these last several years.

Most importantly, I owe *Real Friends Talk About Race* to the BIPOC friends, authors, and educators I've learned from, without whom I could not have written this book. Your wisdom guides me, expands me, and humbles me. Thank you.